DEADLY DEEDS!

A compilation of
Buckinghamshire murder cases

Len Woodley

To my wife Mary,
for her love, patience and support
over many years.

By the same author:
Murder in Buckinghamshire
Buckinghamshire Murders
The Last Patrol - Policemen killed on duty while serving in the
Thames Valley

First published September 2003
by
The Book Castle
12 Church Street
Dunstable
Bedfordshire LU5 4RU

ISBN 1 903747 38 4

Typeset and Designed by Priory Graphics
Flitwick, Bedfordshire
Printed by Antony Rowe Ltd.
Bumper's Farm, Chippenham, Wiltshire SN14 6LH

Contents

About the Author

Leonard Woodley was born in Slough. On leaving school he joined the then Buckinghamshire Constabulary and served for the next thirty-three years at various stations in the county. On retirement, he worked for the High Sheriff of Buckinghamshire and then for British Waterways as a Patrol officer. On leaving that job he became a temporary Coroner's Officer for Milton Keynes. Now fully retired, he researches old murders and the story of policing in Bucks. He lives with his wife Mary in the New City area.

Sources

BOOKS:

'Perfect Murder' by Bernard Taylor & Stephen Knight. Grafton Books 1988.

'Forty Years of Murder' by Sir Keith Simpson. Harrap 1978.

'The Hanslope Park Tragedy' by Lieut. Col.The Honourable Edward Gerald French D.S.O. The Hove Shirley Press 1968.

'The History of Slough' by Maxwell Fraser. Slough Corporation 1973.

NEWSPAPERS:

Slough Observer; Windsor, Slough & Eton Express; Buckingham Advertiser; Bucks Examiner; Bucks Herald; Bucks Free Press; Amersharn & Chesham Advertiser; Illustrated Police News; News of the World; The Sun; The Daily Mirror.

Acknowledgements

Once again 1 have been helped by many people who willingly gave their time to answer my many enquiries regarding the various murders described in this book. 1 owe them all a great deal and 1 gladly take this opportunity to thank them very much. The following all "assisted me with my enquiries". Ex Detective Inspector Peter Burrows, ex Detective Superintendent Roger Sillence, ex Detective Constable Brian Bedwell, Superintendent Frank Sullivan, ex P.C. Barrie Jones and former Police Constable Alan Rentell who were very helpful when 1 was researching the "Incredible Hulk" murders. Ex Detective Sergeant Tony Dale patiently answered my queries, showed me the various newspaper articles concerning the Dr.Davidson murder and took me to the scene of the atrocious crime. Ex Inspector John Pearson was also most helpful with his reminiscences about this tragically unsolved murder.

Other retired members of the Thames Valley Police who were invaluable in their assistance regarding the various killings in and around High Wycombe were ex Superintendent Ray Tilly, ex Detective Sergeant Peter Apted, ex Inspector Stuart Ayres and former Constables, Jim Cuming and David Binns. My friend and colleague in the Police for many years, Derek Edmonds, once again looked through his vast collection of photographs to supplement the illustrations in this book. I would also like to thank former Superintendent Stuart Jones for his assistance whilst I was writing the Stocklake murder. Two former Detective Superintendents who also advised me were Roger Nicklin regarding the Deidre Sainsbury murder and Anthony Miller on the dreadful murder of Mrs Barrett. 1 would like to state my appreciation of Jane Bird and Iris Garrett of Slough Museum, who, as usual, searched and found for me photographs of old Slough. My thanks also go to the then British Railways Board for permission to use a print of the first Slough Railway Station that the poisoner, John Tawell, left in such a hurry in 1845, only to return a day or so later in handcuffs, to Sergeant Phillip Trendall of the British Transport Police History Society who explained the workings and uniform of the early Great Western Railway Police, and to Mrs Evelyn Playle of Aldeby in Suffolk who showed me the church of that quiet village and who explained the roots of the Tawell family to me, one quiet Saturday afternoon. My thanks also go to Matthew Barrow of the Science Museum for explaining the intricacies of the early electric telegraph machine installed at Slough. Michael Shaw, Constable of the Thames Valley Police, who, in his research into the members of the former Bucks Constabulary, was most helpful in being able to produce a number of photographs of Police activity at the Squire Watts' murder. I was also greatly assisted by Roger Drage of the Milton Keynes Museum, who has thoroughly investigated the murder that occurred that pre Great War summer's day, as I was by Don Hellings of Hanslope.

My thanks go to John Grace, Police Constable for many years in North Bucks, who took me around Steeple Claydon where the sad murder of an infant disturbed the tranquillity of that village in the nineteenth century.

Once again, the staff at the County Reference Library at Aylesbury were most helpful as they were at the newspaper Library at Colindale, and at the Slough, Staines, High Wycombe, Milton Keynes and Buckinghamshire Libraries.

Finally my thanks go to my wife Mary, who accompanied me around many scenes of murders and several churchyards.

If I have missed out anyone, I hope they will excuse my forgetfulness.

Introduction

Within this book, I have presented a further collection of murders from the County of Buckinghamshire. They range from the mid-Victorian poisoner, who murdered his mistress and attempted to escape justice by catching the train to London, and might have done so had it not been for another technological invention; to the late twentieth century, when a young mother innocently allowed her murderer into her house. They show the rather haphazard approach to law and order in the early years of the nineteenth century compared with the hard working teams that investigate murder and serious crime at the present time. One thing that never alters however, that all the murders shows human nature at its worst.

EXECUTION

OF JOHN TAWELL,

AND FULL CONFESSION, TO HIS WIFE, IN A LETTER

Of the Murder of Sarah Hart.

Aylesbury,
This morning, 8 o'clock.

At an early hour this morning, the sheriffs, with their usual attendants, arrived at the prison, and after partaking of some refreshment, proceeded to the condemned cell, where they found the reverend ordinary engaged in prayer with the wretched culprit.

After the usual formalities had been observed of demanding the delivery of the body of the prisoner into their custody, Tawell was conducted to the press-room, where his irons were struck off. The executioner, with his assistants, then commenced pinioning his arms, which operation they skilfully and quickly despatched. During these awful preparations he sighed deeply, but uttered not a word. At a quarter before 8, all the arrangements having been completed, the bell of the prison commenced tolling, and the melancholy procession was formed:—the reverend ordinary, preceding the culprit on his way to the fatal drop, began reading in a distinct tone, the burial service for the dead. No sound, if we except the deep sighs of the unhappy man, interrupted the clergyman, as the procession moved along the subterranean passage. On arriving at the steps leading to the scaffold, he turned round, and tremulously thanked the sheriffs and the worthy governor of the prison, for their kind attentions to him during his confinement. Then, firmly but with a slow motion, he ascended the scaffold, on reaching which he was placed in the necessary position. Whilst the executioner was adjusting the fatal apparatus of death, which was done in an incredibly short space of time, Tawell was deeply absorbed in prayer. The executioner, having drawn the cap over his face, retired from the scaffold; and, on the signal being given, the bolt was withdrawn, and the unhappy man was launched into eternity. A few convulsive struggles were perceptible, and he ceased to exist. After hanging the usual time, the body was cut down, and conveyed into the prison.

Wednesday, March 12.

At 10 o'clock the judges took their seats upon the bench, at the Court-house, Aylesbury; and shortly afterwards the prisoner was brought in. The indictment having been read, accusing John Tawell with the murder of Sarah Hart, the counsel for the prosecution opened the case, and called the following witnesses.

Mary Anne Ashley—I live in Bath Place, Salt Hill. On the 1st of January I saw the prisoner enter deceased's house, which was next door to mine; and between six and seven in the evening I heard a stifled sort of scream, and saw the prisoner coming out of Mrs. Hart's house. I said, I am afraid my neighbour is ill; but the prisoner, who appeared agitated, made no reply. When I got inside her door, deceased was lying on the floor, with her petticoats nearly up to her knees, and the left stocking was down and a bun. I found nothing deleterious, but I found proofs of the presence of prussic acid in the contents of the stomach. I spoke to her, but she made no reply. Froth came from the corners of her mouth, and she appeared to be dying. I went to the landlady's, (Mrs. Wheeler's), the last house in the row, and Mrs. Burrett, a relative of Mrs. Wheeler's, returned with me. We placed a pillow on the child's chair, and put deceased's head upon it, and sent for Dr. Champneys. On Mrs. Hart's table, when I first went in, there was a bottle, and a glass with some porter, and another glass with only a little froth in it. Deceased spoke, as deceased's house. Prisoner came a little froth in it. Deceased spoke, as previously to the scream, in rather an undertone, but only a few words. Mr. J. Cooper—I am a practical chemist, and was formerly lecturer on chemical jurisprudence. Mr. bason full. ill; but the prisoner, who appeared called on me and requested a bottle, another bottle with some got inside her door, deceased was a loud tone, but only a few words, some stout with deceased, and the considerable sum in that line, and latter presently after became very entered into several trading transactions, and, as my child was of a human guilty, and the judge pronounced sentence of death upon him.

Copy of a Letter from the Prisoner to his Wife.

"My dear Wife,
"I pray thee to forgive the injury I have done thee. If thou wilt pray for me, my dear, for my soul shall be redeemed by the Holy Spirit, let thy wretched husband's misery cause thee to pray for him. That I did commit the horrid crime I now confess, and I also made the attempt last September. I am, dear wife, your wretched husband,
"JOHN TAWELL."

He was transported to Sydney for possessing a forged Bank of England note, where his good conduct obtained for him emancipation. Knowing something of chemistry, he soon amassed a considerable sum in this line of

actions. After living 15 years in Sydney, he returned home, where he has been endeavouring to gain admittance as a member of the Society of Friends; to which body he belonged before his transportation, but they would not admit him. During his first wife's illness, the deceased nursed her, whence arose their illicit correspondence.

COPY OF VERSES.

GOOD people all of each degree
Attend to what I shall unfold.
It is a dreadful tragedy
Will make your very blood run cold.
Your hearts alas with grief will bleed,
When you this cruel tale shall hear;
There's not been done so vile a deed
Since the days of Courvoisier.

John Tawell is my name 'tis true,
In wealth and splendour once I've dwelt,
A hypocrite I've always been,
Nor meek ey'd mercy never felt.
My first crime was Forgery,
A convict was to Sidney sent,
I riches gain'd oh! misery,
My stubborn heart did not relent.

To lustful passions I gave way,
At virtue I had always smiled.
Poor Sarah Hart I did betray,
She by me had proved with child,
My house she left, yet still the same,
In adulterous love we pass'd our time,
In unholy deeds of guilt and shame:
My vile unconscious of our crime.

Two smiling babes by her she bore,
Oh! what a wretch thus to betray
Her from the paths of virtue tore.
And then to take her life away!
To Salt-hill in Buckinghamshire,
Poor Sarah Hart, the did remove,
There I to her did oft repair,
To carry on our guilty love.

Grown tired at last, yet full of grief,
Oh God! poor thing, I did her slay,
With prussic acid poison vile,
I took her harmless life away.
While she her glass had pledg'd to me
And drank my health for many a year,
Oh! what a monster I must be,
With poison I had drugg'd her beer.

Cut off in life, sent to the tomb,
With all her sins upon her head,
Would I could recall her doom,
And raise her once more from the dead,
For none had seen my victim fall,
For none to save or help was nigh,
Yet one above had witnessed all,
'Twas God's allseeing, piercing eye.

I was taken, tried and cast,
My gold in hundreds flew amain:
To save my life all hope is past,
My gold also, was all in vain,
And I must die in ignominy,
For death in terror now I wait,
O shun that crime, adultery,
Take warning by a murderer's fate.

Next Friday I am doomed to die,
While gaping thousands round appear
Some will heave a pitying sigh,
Nor for the murderer drop a tear.
Back, back! they come! I hear their time,
The executioner now I see,
I'll soon be number'd with the dead,
Great God of mercy pardon me.

Distant view of the cottage where the murder was committed, Bath Place, Salt Hill.

J, Paul & Co., Printers, (Successors to the late J, Catnach) 2 & 3, Monmouth-court, Seven Dials.

X

'DRESSED IN THE GARB OF A KWAKER!'

Slough - 1845

John Tawell was born in Aldeby, Norfolk, in 1784, but as soon as he was able to he left that quiet village and made his way by ferry and track to the coast, where he entered the service of a Quaker lady, who kept a shop near Lowestoft. He worked well, for it is said that he gained the confidence of his employer and the respect of her customers. He attempted to join the Society of Friends[1], and he also, unfortunately, made the acquaintance of one Joseph Hunton. Hunton would be executed some years later for forgery and it might well be that he exercised some malign influence over young Tawell, who would, some years later, himself fall foul of the law.

Tawell moved to London where he worked for a while in a linen drapery. He was now in his early twenties and, having a young man's normal sexual appetites, it was not long before he had seduced one of the domestic servants where he was employed. A wedding was hastily arranged and the new Mrs. Tawell was eventually to bear two sons. Tawell now became a salesman for a drug manufacturer and was so employed for the next seven years, learning a considerable amount about medicines, drugs and poisons. This career unfortunately came to a sudden end in 1814, when he was apprehended and charged with forging banknotes. He was in dire peril of his life, as certain types of forgery were capital offences. However, reasoning that as the bank the notes were drawn on was a Quaker bank and Quakers are opposed to the taking of life, Tawell pleaded guilty to possession only. This was a non-capital offence and the bank accepted his plea.

Tawell was sentenced to seven years imprisonment, but having argued so strongly that he would not survive such a term in this country, he was instead sentenced to fourteen years transportation at the Convict Establishment in New South Wales. On his arrival in Sydney, Tawell was sent, not to do the hard menial work like the

---

1 Whether he actually did or not is disputed.

other convicts, but instead to become an assistant in one of the hospitals, his knowledge of drugs having been recognised by the authorities. By showing due diligence to his work over a number of years, Tawell's superiors recommended to the Governor of the Colony that he be given a ticket of leave, and shortly after he was granted his freedom.

Tawell now set himself up in his own shop, becoming one of the most prosperous men in Sydney. All good things come to an end, and Mrs Tawell, hearing of her husband's good fortune and desiring to see him again, for she had received precious little in the long intervening years, set sail for Australia, a subscription having been raised for her. Absence does not always make the heart grow fonder, for Tawell, believing that he had left England behind for good, had taken a mistress. Nonetheless, Mrs. Tawell settled in the new home and her husband continued successfully with his business and completed the education of his sons.

In 1831, Tawell decided that he would return to England. He had accumulated something in the region of between £40-60,000, a not inconsiderable amount in those days. That he was well thought of in the colony was evident when a party was thrown in his honour upon his leaving. He was not completely finished in Australia, for he journeyed back there for various transactions which netted him several thousand more pounds, but, when one of his sons died, he severed all connections with New South Wales.

The Tawells now settled in Greenwich, but Mrs. Tawell had been in poor health for some time, and her husband engaged a nurse, Sarah Hart, to look after her. Mrs. Tawell died and Sarah Hart became the mistress of Tawell. (Whether or not any impropriety had taken place before the demise of Mrs. Tawell is not known.) Sarah bore him two more children, a girl and a boy.

Tawell now met and soon married another lady in 1841, obviously refusing to do the right thing by Sarah. He moved to Berkhamsted in Hertfordshire and lived it up in some style. Sarah, becoming somewhat of an encumbrance, was given an allowance of £1 per week. She continued to live in London for some time afterwards and became known as 'Mrs. Hart', 'to preserve her respectability'. Tawell visited her quarterly to pay her the allowance. Sarah explained to her neighbours that her husband was abroad and that the gentleman who visited was a friend of her husband.

Sarah then moved to a cottage in the country at Salt Hill, near to the small town of Slough in Buckinghamshire, where Tawell visited her every three months to pay her maintenance. In September 1843, after one particular visit made by Tawell, she became violently ill after consuming some stout paid for by her former lover. She recovered, and the matter was, for the time being, forgotten.

Fifteen months passed by, and on the afternoon of Wednesday, January 1st, 1845 John Tawell called at the Jerusalem Coffee-house in Cornhill in the city of London. He asked a waiter what time the coffee-house closed and, when told, said that he intended to leave his greatcoat there whilst he went to the West End. He would collect the garment later that evening. In fact, he went to the Great Western Railway terminus at Paddington and boarded the 4pm train to Slough. Upon his arrival there, he made his way to Bath Place at Salt Hill where Sarah Hart lived.

About 6.30pm Sarah called at the nearby Windmill Tap and asked for a bottle of Guinness. She remained there for about ten minutes, chatting to the barmaid, Catherine White. As she left she asked if she could borrow a corkscrew with which to open the bottle. White loaned her one and Sarah, gathering up both items, walked out of the door and headed back to her cottage. On her way she passed a gardener, named Barlow, to whom she explained her haste by saying that she had a friend who had called in and she had been to fetch a little stout for him. Barlow nodded and saw her open the front door of her cottage and enter it.

A few minutes later, Mrs. Mary Ann Ashley, also of Bath Place, heard a scream coming from Sarah's cottage next door. Curiosity overcame her and, taking a lighted candle, she made her way in the direction of her neighbour's dwelling. As she approached, she saw a man looking like a Quaker coming down the path of Sarah Hart's cottage. Both Mrs. Ashley and the man reached the gate at the same time. To Mrs. Ashley he appeared confused and very shaken and had trouble opening the gate, and she had to assist him. She asked him what was the matter with Sarah. He stared back at her very hard, but made no reply. Mrs. Ashley walked past the man and, as she walked up the path to Sarah's front door, she glanced over her shoulder and noticed the rather strange man now striding along the road towards Slough.

As soon as she entered the cottage, Mrs. Ashley could see that there was something radically wrong with Sarah. She lay groaning on the floor with her clothes in some disarray. She asked Sarah what had happened, but received no coherent response and, by now being thoroughly alarmed, she sent for the local doctor, Dr. Champneys, who lived nearby. When he arrived a few minutes later, he thought he could detect a faint pulse, but, before he could do anything, Mrs. Hart died.

A number of other persons now attended the cottage including the local constable,[2] to whom the doctor entrusted the body of the deceased pending a full post-mortem examination. He was also given the care of the, by now, empty bottle of Guinness, a glass and a broken phial, which the doctor had found in the fireplace.

Another person who visited the scene was the Reverend Edward Thomas Champneys, a cousin of the doctor, who was informed of the circumstances surrounding the mysterious death and also that a man, thought to be a Quaker, had left the house shortly before the discovery of the body. Knowing that a train was leaving shortly for London, the Rev. Champneys hastily made for Slough Railway Station. Upon reaching there he observed a Quaker boarding the train and suspected that he was the man who had been seen to leave Sarah Hart's cottage. The man, however, appeared eminently respectable, dressed as he was as a Quaker gentleman, and the Rev. Champneys hesitated to detain him. Before he could make his mind up, the train pulled out of Slough Railway Station and began its journey to London. Champneys spoke to the Stationmaster, Howell, about the affair. That worthy man disagreed with Champneys' reasoning. Champneys began to realise that perhaps he had been

2 *This was before the formation of the Bucks Constabulary.*

4

wrong not to have detained the man. He confided to Howell that all appeared lost, for the prime suspect had boarded the train, which was now on its way to the capital, where the man would alight and vanish into the Great Metropolis, perhaps for ever.

Howell smiled and suggested that perhaps the reverend gentleman might like to try the newly installed electric telegraph, which connected Slough Railway Station to Paddington. Perhaps a message could be sent alerting the authorities and they could detain the suspect upon his arrival. Howell and the Rev. Champneys quickly drafted a message to be sent. 'A murder has just been committed at Salt Hill and the suspected murderer was seen to take a first class ticket for London by the train which left Slough at 7.42pm. He is in the garb of a...' The telegraph had no provision for the letter 'Q'. Both men thought the matter over and decided to spell the next word phonetically. Therefore the message continued, 'He is in the garb of a kwaker...he is in the last compartment of the second first class carriage.'

Both men now waited eagerly for the reply. It came sometime later from the Paddington operator. 'The up train has arrived and a person answering in every respect the description given by telegraph came out of the compartment mentioned. I pointed the man out to Sergeant Williams. The man got into a New Road omnibus and Sergeant Williams into the same.' If the two men at Slough Railway Station had anticipated the immediate detention of their man as he alighted at Paddington, they were to be disappointed when they read over the reply, noting that Sergeant Williams had not arrested the suspect but had merely followed him onto a bus!

Sergeant Williams was a member of the Great Western Railway Police which had been formed under the Great Western Railway Act, 1835. This act allowed the company to apply to local justices for 'Special Constables' to be appointed to act, 'within the said railway and other works and every other part thereof.' Upon their formation, the Great Western Railway Police were under the command of an Inspector and numbered some 40 men. Wearing a uniform not unlike that of the Metropolitan Police but with scarlet stand up collars which

Slough Railway Station, whence Tawell left in a hurry.

bore the letters GWR and their number, these Policeman were to be seen in the vicinity of the stations owned by the railway company to which they belonged. Although their powers were strictly limited to the stations, they were however called upon to police the 'New' town of Swindon to prevent damage and keep order. It was not until many years later that their powers of arrest were extended to beyond the environs of the Railway Stations.

Williams must have pondered upon his course of action when shown the telegraph message that had been sent from Slough. Should he detain the suspect on his arrival? There were no directions to do so. He decided that the best course of action would be to remove his distinctive uniform and don a coat and follow the man to his abode.

As Tawell alighted from his carriage and boarded the omnibus, Williams followed him, even at one stage collecting his fare from Tawell who, completely unaware of his 'shadow', left the bus near the Bank of England and made his way to the Coffee-house where he had left his great coat earlier. He then continued to a lodging house in Southwark kept by the Society of Friends. Sergeant Williams had followed his man all the way and now, deciding that Tawell was settled for the night, returned to Paddington.

The next day, Williams, perhaps with further, more explicit instructions, decided to seek the assistance of the Metropolitan Police. After explaining the situation to Inspector Wiggins of D.Divison, both men set out for Southwark. When they entered the lodgings they found that Tawell had left! It would be understandable if Williams felt a certain uneasiness at the thought that perhaps he had let a suspected murderer slip through his fingers.

The two Policemen now made their way to the Jerusalem Coffee-house, in the forlorn hope that perhaps their quarry might just be there. They opened the door and there to their no doubt immense relief they saw Tawell sitting nonchalantly. Inspector Wiggins was made of sterner stuff than either the Rev. Champneys or his Railway Police colleague and went straight up to his man. He asked the

'Quaker' gentleman if he had been to Slough the previous day.

"No,' Tawell replied. "I did not leave town all day yesterday."

Wiggins was satisfied. Placing a hand upon Tawell's shoulder, and putting an end to all the indecision that had so far dogged the case, he informed Tawell that he would be arrested on suspicion of murdering Sarah Hart. Tawell drew himself up, "Thee must be mistaken in the identity. My station in society places me above suspicion."

Wiggins was not overawed by Tawell's manner and detained him, conveying him to the Inquest that was being held at Salt Hill, where he produced Tawell as a conjuror would pull a rabbit from a hat. For two days the Coroner and his jury listened to what the witnesses had to say. Catherine White, who recalled Sarah popping in for a bottle of Guinness; William Barlow, who had seen Sarah scuttling off back to her cottage, and her death; and Mrs. Ashley, who had encountered Tawell as he made off whilst she tried to comfort Sarah in her death throes.

At the close of the first day's hearing Tawell applied for bail, saying that, as he was the Town Surveyor for Berkhamsted, he had a public situation to fill and his appearance at the Inquest seriously interrupted his performance of those duties. He pledged his word that, if given bail, he would re-attend on the date chosen for the adjourned Inquest. The Coroner declined to take that course of action, and remanded him into the custody of Superintendent Perkins of the Eton Police. However, he directed Perkins to 'afford his prisoner every comfort compatible with his standing in society.'

Whilst in the custody of Perkins, Tawell talked about Sarah Hart, telling the Superintendent, in the presence of two other witnesses, that she had been in his service for over two years, adding, "I was pestered with letters from her whilst I was in London and I determined to give her no more money. She was a bad woman. A very bad woman. She said she would make away with herself if I did not give her any money. I went down to her house and told her I would not give her any more money. She asked me to give her a drop of porter. She had a glass and I had a glass. She held in her hand, over the glass, a very small phial and said, "I will! I will!" She poured something out of the phial into the stout and drank part of it. She then lay down on the rug and I walked out. I should not have gone out if I had thought she had been in earnest. I certainly should not have left her." The importance of this statement, coming as it did after Tawell had denied being in Slough, was not lost on the Superintendent. At the close of the second day's hearing the Coroner's jury returned a verdict of wilful murder against Tawell, who was now committed for trial.

He appeared at Buckinghamshire Assizes in March before Baron Parks, and for the duration of the trial, which lasted for three days, the courtroom was packed. The murder and subsequent arrest had caught the public's imagination. Tawell, on his part was certain that he would be acquitted, so certain in fact that he arranged for a carriage to be waiting outside the Court.

All the witnesses, especially the medical ones, were listened to with great attention by everyone in the court. Dr. Champneys told of how he had attended Sarah Hart on the evening of January 1st. He had felt for a pulse but could not find any and believed that she was dead. The next day he had performed a post-mortem examination on the deceased. As he opened her body, he could smell prussic acid. Removing the stomach and contents, he took them, together with the bottle of Guinness, a half eaten bun, a glass tumbler and the phial found in the room where Mrs. Hart had died, to an analytical chemist in London.

Mr. Cooper, the analytical chemist to whom the doctor had conveyed his samples gave long and detailed evidence on the next day of the trial regarding the tests he had carried out on the various samples presented to him. He had found that Mrs. Hart had indeed died from the administration of prussic acid and, producing the various items that had been submitted to him, caused a great stir in Court. A chemist from the City identified Tawell as having purchased a bottle of prussic acid from his shop in the early afternoon before the murder had occurred, ostensibly for the treatment of varicose veins.

Tawell's defence lawyer attempted to show that Mrs. Hart had eaten a number of apples on January 1st, and that she had also consumed the pips, which contained prussic acid, and had, albeit unwittingly, contributed to her own demise. (She would have had to have eaten an inordinate amount of pips to have the amount of prussic acid found in her stomach, it was pointed out.) Henceforth, Tawell's lawyer was known by the sobriquet, 'Applepip' Kelly.

In a long summing up, the Judge disposed of this argument and pointed out that Tawell had not only had the wherewithal to commit murder, the prussic acid purchased in London, but he also had the motive, the expense of paying Sarah Hart £13 a quarter for the upkeep of herself and her children. He further urged the jury not to forget that Tawell had offered several different stories to the authorities. When detained by Inspector Wiggins, he was adamant that he had not been to Slough, but, whilst quartered with Superintendent Perkins during the Inquest, he stated that he had been visiting his former lover and she had committed suicide.

The jury were absent for only half-an-hour before deciding that Tawell was guilty, and Baron Parks, after denouncing him for his hypocrisy for adopting the dress of a virtuous, peaceful, benevolent and religious body of persons, passed sentence of death upon him.

Two weeks later, on Friday, 29th March, before a large crowd assembled in the Market Square at Aylesbury, John Tawell was hanged. It was to be the last time that an execution was to take place in front of the Assize court building.[3] Tawell left a full confession of his guilt with the Prison Chaplain.

A few months after the trial and execution had taken place, it was said that some people were travelling in the carriage of a train from Paddington to Slough. For almost the entire length of the journey no-one spoke, when suddenly a man seated in the corner of the carriage pointed at the telegraph wires as they ran alongside the railway track and is supposed to have remarked, "Them's the cords that hanged John Tawell."

3 *It is still used today, as the Crown Court.*

10

"ANNE, FETCH ME A KNIFE!"

Steeple Claydon - 1871

The village of Steeple Claydon lies just a few miles from the old County town of Buckingham. Although much built on in recent years it still retains to a great extent the tranquillity it has preserved over the centuries. Its one claim to fame is that Oliver Cromwell slept here during the Civil War before attacking nearby Hillesden House and burning it to the ground. However, in 1871 the residents were disturbed by a crime so horrific that it was a considerable time before the village could return to its more normal, peaceful state.

In the census returns for 1871, Steeple Claydon was reported as having 211 inhabited houses and eight uninhabited; it had 447 male persons and 489 females. They were shown to be of various rural occupations; farmer, farm labourer, sweep, lace maker, blacksmith, servant etc.

The village was in that year the headquarters of the northwestern Division of the Buckinghamshire Constabulary and Superintendent Benjamin Shepherd was stationed here with one Constable. At one house in the village called Camp Farm there lived two sisters, Miss Mary Emma and Miss Sarah Fanny Macdonald and shown as boarding with them were the Logan children, David, eight years, Ethel, 6 years, Bruce, 5 years and Ross, 4 years. Also living at Camp Farm were the following servants, Catherine Muir, a nurse and a native of Bothwell in Scotland, Anne Smith, a housemaid born in the County of Wiltshire and Elizabeth White, the cook who came from Little Tew, Oxfordshire. Not shown but also employed by the Misses Macdonald was Anne Ladyman, 19 years old, an assistant nursemaid. She had been born in the village, lived with her parents and worked at Camp Farm on mornings only.

Mr.Logan, the father of the children boarded with the Macdonald sisters, was an engineer with the Peninsula and Oriental Company and was currently based in Bombay. He had wanted his wife to join him there but she was reluctant to leave her children in England

West Street, Steeple Claydon.

Steeple Claydon

whilst her husband did not wish to inflict the heat of India upon his offspring. When Mrs.Logan lost her fifth and youngest child in 1870, she decided that she would join her husband after all. It was to prove a fatal decision.

For a number of years she had employed Mrs. Muir as a nursemaid and was quite satisfied with her. Mrs.Muir it appears had lost her husband and her children and no doubt looked upon the Logan boys and girl as surrogates.

When Mrs.Logan decided to join her husband she looked around for somewhere to place her children and found that the Macdonald household at Steeple Claydon appeared to suit admirably. Leaving them there, still with Mrs.Muir as their nurse but with the Misses Macdonald in overall charge, Mrs.Logan left this country for India. In September of 1870, David went to boarding school at Reading leaving his brothers and sister at Camp Farm.

All seemed to be going smoothly at the house, the children played and attended classes with the two Macdonald sisters. They in turn appeared to be getting along with the nurse, Mrs. Muir. In the spring of 1871, however Catherine Muir was not quite the same person as she used to be and matters had become a little fraught between the Macdonalds and the children's nurse. On Monday, 1st May, Mary Macdonald heard Bruce being slapped and then scream. She went to the nursery and asked Catherine Muir what the trouble was. Catherine replied that the boy had spilt water on the carpet and she had rebuked him by slapping him with her hand.

A week passed by and after breakfast one morning Mary Macdonald saw Mrs. Muir with the children's outdoor clothes and enquired as to the reason for this. Mrs. Muir replied that she proposed taking the children for a walk, adding that she had promised that they could go into the garden that afternoon with their toys and play. As Miss Macdonald had intended to give them lessons, she was just a little put out.

The children's aunts came to Camp Farm the next day and Mary had a long conversation with them about the care of the three children. When the aunts concluded their visit they were accompanied to the Railway Station by Mary and Catherine but not before the nurse had gone to a cupboard and poured herself a glass of beer and drank it. One can imagine the pursed lips and knowing looks that passed between the ladies as this little scenario was enacted.

After the departure of the aunts Mary heard Ross crying in the nursery and on going upstairs and trying to gain entry found that the door was locked. "Muir,"she called out, "are you there?"

"Yes," replied the nurse.

Mary rattled the door knob impatiently, "I want to give the little boys their garden seeds", she explained.

Catherine opened the door slightly, "You can't give them to them now because they have gone to bed."

To Mary this was a most unusual practise and there was a minor squabble between the two women about this.

Mary and Catherine had a talk in which the nurse was informed that she had to leave Camp Farm because of her intemperate language and wilful defiance. Miss Macdonald emphasised that Catherine was not being dismissed from Mrs.Logan's employment but she simply could not be allowed to remain with the children at Camp Farm until she, Mary, had corresponded with their parents and had heard back from them.

Catherine had wept when she was told this and said that she had promised Mrs.Logan that she would never leave the children. When she had calmed down, Catherine had asked when she was to leave and was informed that she would have to go on Thursday which was just a few days hence. She was to go to Eltham to Mrs.Logan's sister.

Shortly after this conversation had taken place Mary told Ethel Logan to go upstairs but the little girl had refused unless one of the Macdonald sisters accompanied her. When the child had been asked why she answered, "Muir is there, she will beat me."

That night, Catherine walked round to the local doctor's house. Dr.Somerset was out and she spoke instead to his wife. Catherine explained that she wanted some laudanum to assuage a pain that she had in her side and she was duly handed a rather large quantity, 2ozs; enough, it was pointed out later to poison not only herself but also the children in her care. When Dr.Somerset returned and his young wife explained what had occurred he sent her post haste to Camp Farm with instructions to warn Mrs.Muir of the danger she was in with the amount she had been given. Mrs. Somerset spoke to Catherine and was handed some but not all of the laudanum; it was later ascertained that the nurse had poured a certain amount into another bottle which she retained.

Mary Macdonald, when she found out about this was most concerned, but Catherine sought to calm her fears by applying some of the laudanum to her supposedly injured side.

The next day Catherine was not in a very good humour as she packed ready to leave. Elizabeth, the cook, remarked that Anne, the assistant nursemaid, would think it strange when she found out that Catherine was leaving. "Oh!" responded Mrs.Muir, "she will get a worse fright than that."

As she did not explain what she meant by that remark Elizabeth merely shrugged and went about her chores.

That afternoon, Catherine sent the housemaid out for a bottle of brandy, giving her 6/- to purchase it with. It was for her brother who was not well, she said by way of explanation.

Thursday, the day of departure, dawned and Anne Ladyman arrived at Camp Farm. When she went upstairs she was somewhat surprised to find Catherine Muir still in bed; she usually slept with Ross and the children asleep. Anne carried on and returned a little later and saw Ethel sitting on the floor dressing. Catherine stirred and, after asking the time, enquired if Bruce was awake. Anne replied that he was just waking. Catherine then rose and sat on the fender of the fireplace and said quietly, "Anne, get me a knife."

The young woman offered her a penknife which Catherine refused, saying she wanted a tableknife. Anne went downstairs, found a tableknife and took it back to Catherine, who proceeded to cut the garter off her stocking. Anne once more left the bedroom.

Mary Macdonald was by now rather concerned at the non-appearance of the children and sent the housemaid, Anne Smith, to find out what was keeping them. Smith soon returned, excitedly telling her employer that both boys were still in bed and the room reeked of brandy. Mary decided that it was time that she paid a visit to find out exactly what was going on. Entering the bedroom she saw Ross sitting up in his bed. "Nanna very sick," he said innocently, adding, "Bruce very sick."

"Rossy, have you been sick?" she enquired.

"No," the boy replied.

Miss Macdonald glanced across at the next bed and what she saw made her dash out of the room, for it was saturated in blood and Bruce appeared to be seriously injured. She clutched the top of the stairs for support and called out to her brother-in-law, the Reverend Charles Plumtre, who was staying at Camp Farm. He ran up the stairs at his sister-in-law's frantic cry. He saw the same awful sight and immediately sent for the local doctor and the Police.

When Dr. Somerset attended he realised that the boy was beyond all human aid, for his throat had been cut from the spine to the windpipe, severing the arteries. As the Police arrived in the shape of Superintendent Shepherd, both he and the doctor saw Catherine Muir crouching on the floor. She had a wild look on her face and she appeared to the two men to be under the influence of the brandy or laudanum or perhaps both. Her clothes, face and hands were spattered with blood.

Superintendent Shepherd brought her to her feet and as he did so he caught sight of the bloodstained tableknife which had lain beneath her. Instructing the women of the house to dress her, the Police Officer looked carefully around the room. He took in the dreadful sight of the dead child, then he noticed the uncorked brandy bottle and the laudanum bottle as well as the penknife. All the time he could hear Catherine rambling on as she was dressed, "Miss Macdonald has been most kind but Fanny has not."

When she was dressed she was taken to the Police Station and charged with murder. After making arrangements for her to be watched over by a female, the Superintendent returned to Camp

Farm and collected the various items relating to the killing and which he knew would be needed as exhibits at any subsequent Court proceedings. He also found a letter that Catherine had written to her sister. This read, in part '....I will write you Thursday first if all is well. Don't grieve for my lot in life...forget me my dear sister; on earth I am persecuted.' When he returned to the Police Station, Catherine asked Shepherd if he had found the letter but before he could reply she continued, "If so, they will confirm all...If they had let me live until Mrs.Logan had returned I should not have cared." Superintendent Shepherd, in an honest attempt to sustain her, said, "You are living and will live." "No," sighed his prisoner, "I am not. I know I am dying."

Catherine Muir was swiftly committed for trial and on a July day in 1871 as she waited in the cells beneath the Court, she rubbed shoulders with other prisoners who were also appearing at the Aylesbury Summer Assizes. They were an assorted bunch of criminals charged with a variety of offences. Stealing a flannel shirt of the value of two shillings, obtaining property by means of a forged letter, setting fire to a pig sty, assault, false pretences, stealing ducks, larceny of trusses of hay and one poor woman who was charged with killing her infant son. Such was the state of crime in the County of Buckingham in mid-Victorian times.

Catherine Muir was taken up to the dock and pleaded "Not Guilty", to the charge of murder. After the case for the prosecution had been outlined, Mary Macdonald was sworn and told of giving notice to the prisoner to quit her premises on Thursday, May 11th and the background behind it. Under cross-examination she admitted that Mrs.Logan thought very highly of Catherine and had given her presents, such as a watch and a desk amongst other things for showing great kindness to her children. When Mrs.Logan had sailed from Southampton to join her husband, Catherine had taken David to see her off. When they had returned the other children were excited and happy to see her again. Miss Macdonald explained that she had written to Mrs.Logan that, "Everyone found Catherine....a very great comfort...in every respect...we are all quite fond of her.'

Mr. Metcalfe, for the defence, then asked her about the prisoner's conduct regarding Ross earlier in the year. "In March," she responded, "Rossie was very ill, he became delirious. Muir carried him about in her arms day and night. She was the only one who could soothe him and she was so dreadfully distressed that I feared she would become ill herself." Mary Macdonald continued that she had felt sorry for her having so many broken nights, as Rossie would not be left alone with anyone except his nurse. She had written at the time regarding the mental state of the nurse, 'Muir seems tolerably well. She had been taking medicine, she has been better but her anxiety for Rossie brought it on again.'

In April, she explained, Catherine had complained of a pain in her side, contracted when Rossie had been ill adding, "...When poorly we find her very much depressed". A few days after this observation, David had gone to his school in Reading and Miss Macdonald had written, "...I think nurse has been a good deal worried lately and it has made her very irritable with all the children."

Miss Macdonald agreed with the prisoner's counsel that until that time she had no complaint with her. In May however, she had decided that because of Catherine's defiant manner and her ill treatment of the children she should be separated from them and had proposed that she go and stay with Mrs. Logan's sister.

Anne Ladyman was the next witness and she said that she had always found Catherine to be perfectly kind to the children. When asked about the slap the nurse had administered to Bruce, she stated, "He was throwing water about the room....she gave him a little slap on his arm, it was nothing to hurt him. I did not see any mark and she slapped him with her open hand."

Anne was next questioned on the alleged 'whipping' of the children. "I heard Miss Macdonald one day tell her (the prisoner) to whip the children for putting beads up their noses and she had struck them with her hand."

Anne was asked about the time when Catherine had been told to leave and replied that she had been greatly upset at the thought and on the day before she was due to go she had broken down and had cried very bitterly, saying, "Oh Anne, it's those girls have done the mischief. They've been telling Miss Macdonald lies about me." Anne had not really understood to whom she was referring.

Miss Fanny Macdonald, the next witness, said that she had not quarrelled with Catherine Muir until Tuesday 9th May, when she had heard her use bad language in the kitchen. She had also refused to let Bruce come for his lessons, saying that she intended taking the children for a walk and she was not going to alter her walk for Miss Macdonald.

Superintendent Shepherd now entered the box and said that when he first encountered the prisoner she had kept repeating, "Will you listen to me? Will you hear what I have to say before I die? Don't blame Miss Macdonald, she has been most kind, but Miss Fanny hasn't been kind and she has been the cause of it all."

Shepherd said that he had arrested Mrs. Muir and he was then asked about her general conduct whilst she had been kept at the Police Station pending her appearances at the Inquest and the Magistrates' Court. He replied that she was "...somewhat strange...she was greatly depressed...and the depression showed itself in mental illness." One of her attendants, he went on, had told him that Mrs. Muir had asked her, "to take away the dead bodies; she could see a lot of dead bodies." When the funeral of Bruce had taken place in Devon, the church bell in the village had been tolled and this had greatly upset the prisoner, so much so that the Superintendent had requested that it should be stopped.

Dr. Somerset then told the Court that he had visited the prisoner and was of the opinion that she was suffering from mental illness.

One of the women who had acted as an attendant to Mrs. Muir whilst she was at the Police Station, said that one night she had suffered from hallucinations and had become quite violent as the realisation of what she had done began to sink in. She had become frenzied and it had taken two women to hold her down.

Transferred to Aylesbury Gaol whilst awaiting trial, the prison doctor had kept her under observation and he stated that the prisoner, "... appeared to be labouring under great mental dejection."

Further witnesses called by the defence at the Assizes testified that Mrs.Muir had become mentally unbalanced by the death of Mrs.Logan's baby in 1870.

This concluded the case and the Court was adjourned until the following morning. When it reconvened, Counsel for the Prosecution rose. He had, he said, carefully studied the evidence presented the previous day and it led him to believe that Catherine Muir had been insane at the time of the murder and that now he would withdraw the prosecution. The judge, Sir Alexander Cockburn concurred and directed the members of the jury to return a formal verdict of 'Not Guilty on the grounds of insanity', which, with a few minutes discussion between themselves, they did.

Mrs. Muir was then led gently away by the wardresses to be taken to a Lunatic Asylum.

EDWARDIAN SUNSET

Hanslope - 1912

The years from the death of Queen Victoria until the outbreak of the First World War are sometimes looked back upon with a certain nostalgia. It is thought of as a generally peaceful era, a time when Great Britain was the greatest power upon this earth and had a mighty Empire on which the sun never set. On the surface, at least, it appeared to be a time of prosperity and achievement. When one had pride in one's country. This 'glittering epoch' was called the 'Edwardian Age', as Edward VII was the monarch for most of those years, although for a few of them, of course, King George V reigned.

Actually, there were undercurrents that threatened this idealised notion, especially towards the end of this period. There were industrial disputes in the coalfields and the docks throughout the country; there were women agitating for the vote; Russian Anarchists not only robbed banks but were also quite prepared to ruthlessly kill Policemen during the course of their actions, before becoming surrounded in an East End of London street. It would take a detachment of Guards to bring an end to the Sidney Street siege. There was trouble in Ireland, and a threatened mutiny in the Army, over the proposed imposition of Home Rule on that island, was only averted by the outbreak of the Great War.

In other matters it appeared that the British were not quite so 'top dog' as they liked to believe. Captain Scott reached the South Pole, only to discover that a Norwegian had beaten him to it. That same year, 1912, the 'unsinkable' ship, R.M.S. Titanic, sailed on her maiden voyage across the Atlantic, encountered an iceberg and promptly sank with huge loss of life. The era was to end in 1914 with the outbreak of the Great War and the huge loss of life, almost a million men from the British Empire alone. Things would never be the same again.

The 'Edwardian Age' was certainly a time of great chasms between the classes. The aristocracy ruled at the very top end of the system and the middle classes aspired to do so. The majority of the people of this country, however, were lumped together as the 'lower orders', who were there to work hard, long hours, usually for a pittance. Many still lived in the awful slums of the cities, which shamed this so-called glittering era.

In rural areas, things went on much as they had done for decades. The Squirearchy were the masters and lorded it over the country areas and people. When the Squire and his lady ventured out, the local men would doff their caps, the women would curtsey, and the local Policeman would salute out of respect as they passed by. All would show great deference to their 'betters'. Everyone 'knew' their place. For a minority of people, it was a grand life indeed.

The summer of 1912 was, according to contemporary sources, a relatively poor one, compared to that of the previous year. June and August were described as being very bad, although most of July, taken altogether, was much better. The temperature reached seventy and sometimes eighty degrees, whilst on one particularly scorching day it actually soared into the nineties!

It was on one of these extremely hot days, Sunday, 21st July, that the Squire of Hanslope and his wife prepared themselves for Divine Service at St. James' Church at nearby Hanslope village.

Edward Hanslope Watts had been the squire since the death of his father in 1853. He had married Sophia Edith, the third daughter of Richard Selby-Lowndes of Elmers, Bletchley in 1868. Sophia was one of a number of sisters so renowned for their beauty that they became known as the 'Eight Belles of Bletchley'. One of Sophia's sisters married a subaltern in the 19th Hussars, John Denton Pinkstone French, who later became a Field Marshal, and eventually the 1st Earl of Ypres.

Squire Watts and his wife had one child, a daughter named Irene, and until she married they all lived at Hanslope Park, a handsome edifice, situated in several acres of rural North Buckinghamshire and which had been in the hands of the Watts family since the eighteenth century. The Watts maintained Hanslope Park with the appropriate number of servants, comprising several domestic staff, a coachman, stable boys and, of course, gamekeepers.

Squire Watts of Hanslope Park.

Until 1910, the Squire had done his own shooting on the estate, but then his son-in-law, Mark Pore, had suggested that he might like to take things easier at his age and employ a gamekeeper. Squire Watts decided to take on the gamekeeper who worked for the Selby-Lowndes at Whaddon Hall. This latter family was related to the Squire through marriage and, presumably, Selby-Lowndes could vouch for his man. However, by employing the man, Farrow, Squire Watts had made a decision that was to prove fatal.

The head gamekeeper on the Hanslope estate, as William Farrow now became, was a short, thick set ex-miner, ex cotton weaver from Lancashire in his mid forties. Quite how he made the transition from the industrial north-west to rural Buckinghamshire has never been satisfactorily explained, but make it he did and he appeared to have settled down to the life reasonably well. He apparently liked a drink, but too many tended to make him bad tempered. He did not 'get on' with the under keeper, Henry Martin, and on more than one occasion his employer had cause to speak to him about his ways.

Then there had been the regrettable incident of Mrs. Watts' dog. The Squire and his wife had recently travelled abroad for several weeks and Farrow had been entrusted with the care of Mrs. Watt's favourite dog, a retriever. On their return from holiday, it was discovered that the dog had died, apparently from neglect. So upset had Mrs. Watts been that she henceforth referred to Farrow as " that murderer!" Unbeknown to everyone concerned, this would be prophetic. High words had been exchanged 'twixt Squire and gamekeeper, the upshot being that Squire Watts had given Farrow a fortnight's notice for 'gross dereliction of duty!'

That this action by the Squire, effectively dismissing his head gamekeeper, would have some impact upon Farrow must be considered highly probable. For where would a man gain a similar position, who, when asked for references, was only able to produce one with such a comment? Farrow's outlook for future employment as a gamekeeper must have looked very bleak indeed. The same would be true for his wife and family, for they would all be turned out of their cottage on the estate and would have to find somewhere else

William Farrow, gamekeeper to the Squire.

to stay. Not so easy in late Edwardian Britain. It was certainly a high price to pay for not looking after M'lady's dog, and for not keeping a civil tongue in his head when spoken to by his betters!

These unfortunate incidents were no doubt at the back of the Squire's mind as he and his wife set out to walk the one and a half miles to church. Even for two quite elderly persons, the prospect of such a stroll to the village and back on a beautiful Summer's day must have seemed very pleasant indeed. As they made their way through the Park on this glorious morning, past the Lodge gates and along the quiet country lane towards the village, the only noises to be heard would be the sounds of the wildlife in the fields, and the pealing of the distant Church bells. Perhaps the odd cyclist 'tore by', but the couple would hardly be disturbed by the noisy cars that now traverse this lovely part of North Bucks. Surely this, as later generations would come to think, was the quintessentially perfect Edwardian summer scene, set in a gentle, rural landscape. It would be the last time that the British countryside would be so peaceful. God was in his heaven and all was right with the world, and everyone was aware that, in these, the opening years of the twentieth century, God was an Englishman.

As the popular hymn stated,

'...The pleasant Summer sun,
The ripe fruits in the garden,
He made them everyone.'

There was no premonition of impending doom to spoil the day.

On their arrival at St. James' Church, the Squire and his lady sat in different pews; Mrs. Watts liked to join in the singing with the choir, whilst her husband, not being the possessor of such a fine voice, climbed the stairs to his private gallery. It may be that he could better view the congregation from this vantage point, and see who from the village attended the Sunday morning service and, probably more important, who did not.

Perhaps, on such a fine day, and this is only conjecture, one of the

Hanslope Park.

hymns chosen might have been that same number 573 from the Book of Common Prayer, 'All things bright and beautiful' which also included the verse,

'The rich man in his castle,
The poor man at his gate.
God made them high or lowly,
And order'd their estate.'

And which the entire congregation would sing with no sense of irony.[1]

At the conclusion of the service, the people dispersed to their various homes. Squire Watts and his wife walked languidly back to Hanslope Park, the Squire a little way in front of his wife. It was a leisurely stroll home for the Watts, for, by now, the temperature was in the eighties. They encountered Dr. Rutherford, the local practitioner, cycling towards Hanslope, and they stopped and talked. After a few minutes they resumed their separate ways - the doctor cycling into the village, Squire Watts and his wife sauntering towards the Park. Mrs. Watts again behind her husband and the Squire talking to her over his shoulder, they meandered on, gradually approaching the Park. They were within twenty yards of the lodge gates when suddenly, from a spinney close to the lane, a shotgun was fired a few feet away from the Squire. He took the full blast to his head and fell to the ground, mortally wounded if not already dead. There followed another deafening shot. This time the discharge struck the inert squire in the middle of the back. Mrs. Watts, though all too aware off the man with the shotgun behind the hedge, rushed the few feet to her husband's side. The assassin, seeing that his work was done, made his way off into the spinney.

Mrs. Green, the wife of the coachman, heard the firing, and, on looking out of the lodge window, had seen the squire lying in the road, supported by his wife. She rushed out to offer help and was instructed by Mrs. Watts to fetch a doctor as quickly as she could. George, Mrs. Green's husband, now arrived on the scene and, as he did so, he heard the sound of a further shot coming from the spinney. He noticed that the undergrowth on the edge of it had been trodden

1 *Strangely enough, modern editions have deleted this verse from the hymn.*

Hanslope Church, where Squire Watts worshipped shortly before he was murdered.

down, and he thereupon followed a trail of footprints leading from the verge into the thicket. He had not gone very far when he came upon the body of Farrow, the head gamekeeper. He had used the shotgun on himself!

The Hanslope constable, P.C. Alfred Cooper, on being informed of the incident, hurried to the scene as fast as he could on his cycle. He was used to the more mundane matters that country constables of this period dealt with. The highlights of his usually peaceful existence might include an occasional bout of fowl stealing to solve, or detecting after hours drinking, or even perhaps some poaching from the squire's coverts. Now he had the case of a lifetime to handle! One that seldom happened to other Policemen. Now, perhaps he could shine and show his superior officers that, when demanded, he could deal equally well with a very serious matter such as murder.

The constable had only just arrived, when he heard Green shout, "I've got him." P.C. Cooper thrust his way into the copse and made to where he had heard Green shouting. As he reached the coachman, he saw the lifeless body of Farrow. Cooper bent down and examined the corpse. He observed the barrels of the recently fired shotgun protruding from the mouth of the head gamekeeper, and he could see where the shot fired by Farrow had exited at the rear of his skull, taking the back of his head away with the blast. The constable gingerly took the shotgun from the body and looked carefully at it. He could see that there was still one live cartridge in the gun, whilst another, empty one lay ejected on the ground. Searching the pockets of the gamekeeper's jacket, he came across four more cartridges. As he looked around, the Policeman found another shotgun lying nearby.

Dr. Rutherford, to whom the squire had so recently spoken, had also been summoned to the scene, and cursorily looked over the bodies of the two men, pronouncing them both dead. He was able to say that they had been killed instantaneously. Squire Watts' body was gently removed to the house, as his wife moaned repeatedly, "No, no." Farrow's corpse was taken elsewhere.

An Inquest was opened the following day at a nearby public

At the scene of the murder.

house.[2] Mrs. Watts, who, understandably, was overcome by the violent manner of the death of her husband, was unable to attend and relate the circumstances of her husband's killing. The Chief Constable of Buckinghamshire, Major Otway Mayne, and the Divisional Commander, Superintendent Pearce, attended

No such regard for Mrs. Farrow, the other widow, however, as she was called to give evidence before the Coroner and his jury.[3] She too was very upset by the events of the previous day, but managed eventually to give a coherent account of what had taken place at the Farrow home on Sunday. Her husband, she related, had left the cottage between 10am and 10.30am, saying that he wanted some cartridges for a tenant of the squire. He took the cartridges with him but not a gun. Before leaving the cottage he made an entry in his game-book which he kept in a drawer. When asked by the coroner if her husband had been drinking, Mrs. Farrow replied that he had had a jug full of primrose wine. She had argued with him because he had had nothing to eat the day before. She testified that she had no idea that her husband was under notice to leave the squire's employment, until she had been apprised of this by P.C. Cooper on Sunday night. She added that she had not heard her husband say anything against the squire.

The next witness was Mrs. Beesley, the wife of a tenant farmer on the estate. She told the Inquest that she was a little surprised when Farrow had called at the farm on Sunday morning. He had requested a glass of beer. "To quench his thirst," he had said. Mrs. Beesley had fetched him a half pint, but was uneasy about the look of the man, for in her own words, "...his eyes were glassy, and he did not seem natural."

---

2 *The Greyhound Inn at Tathall End, a hamlet near to Hanslope Park. It is now a private house.*
3 *Inquests were usually held immediately after the sudden death that was being enquired into in those days, but it goes to show the deference shown to a certain class of society, prevalent then, that the Coroner felt he could proceed without calling the prime witness to give evidence. He could have adjourned it, as Coroners usually do nowadays, until Mrs. Watts was able to attend, but chose not to do so.*

The Daily Mirror

THE MORNING JOURNAL WITH THE SECOND LARGEST NET SALE.

No. 2,729.   Registered at the G.P.O. as a Newspaper.   TUESDAY, JULY 23, 1912   One Halfpenny.

BUCKINGHAMSHIRE SQUIRE SHOT DEAD BY A MAD GAMEKEEPER WHILE WALKING HOME FROM CHURCH WITH HIS WIFE.

William Farrow, who committed the murder.

Mr. and Mrs. Watts. The widow was too prostrated with grief to attend yesterday's inquest.

The scene of the crime. Further particulars are given below.—(D.M.P.)

Mr. and Mrs. Mark Poore. Mrs. Poore is Mr. Watts' only daughter.

A terrible tragedy occurred in a country road near Newport Pagnell, in Buckinghamshire. As Mr. Edward Hanslope Watts, a prominent landowner, was walking home from church with his wife he was shot dead by his gamekeeper, William Farrow, who fired two shots from behind a hedge. The man afterwards committed suicide. Mrs. Watts, who is a sister-in-law of General Sir John French, had a narrow escape. In the photograph of the scene of the crime the man on the roadway is seen on the exact spot where Mr. Watts fell. The policeman nearest the telegraph-pole is standing at the place from which the murderer fired.

The murder of the Squire made national headlines.

33

As he slowly drank the beer, Farrow toyed with her husband's gun, which stood inside the front door. Then he suddenly told Mrs. Beesely that he wanted to borrow her husband's razor, as his had gone to be ground. Farrow finished the beer and left the house and an astonished Mrs. Beesley.

The under keeper, Martin, was the next witness and he said that he had seen Farrow on the Saturday night when he had seemed alright. However, in answer to a question from the Coroner, he admitted that in December of the previous year, the head gamekeeper had talked to him of the 'lies' that were being told about him on the estate.

"Mr.Watts was not bought into that, I suppose?" asked the Coroner.

"No," replied Martin.

Dr. Rutherford gave evidence of being summoned to the scene and of inspecting the bodies to ascertain if there was any spark of life left, but had found none. He mentioned in passing that, during the summer of 1911, Farrow had sustained sunstroke, adding that the heat of the day might have produced a sudden apoplectic seizure.

After listening to various other witnesses including Mr. and Mrs. Green and P.C. Cooper and a summing up by the Coroner, the jury returned a verdict of wilful murder against Farrow, who had then committed suicide.

There is a certain element of mystery why Farrow took it into his head to kill the squire. Could it have been because he had been given notice over the affair of the dog and the strong words that had been bandied about between himself and the squire? Or had he, as the doctor had suggested, suffered a seizure and had then killed the squire in a fit of insanity?

It would appear that he had made plans, for apparently it was a rule that the estate gamekeepers were not allowed to carry guns on a Sunday, and so Farrow had planted two shotguns in the spinney where the fatal shooting had taken place. This would be so that he was not seen to be carrying a gun by someone, contrary to the rules.

The funeral cortege of Squire Watts.

Hanslope Church. The vault containing the remains of Squire Watts and his wife.

Although if he intended to take his own life after murdering the squire, why bother with that regulation? He had also taken a number of cartridges with him from his house.

Had he also intended to murder Mrs. Watts at the same time? It can be argued that shooting at such close range as he did, he could hardly have missed the squire's lady if he had wanted to do so. Or did he assume, when he saw her fall down beside her husband's body, that he had shot her too? Again, maybe it was not his intention to injure her at all. All are unanswerable questions.

One of the local newspapers of the time reported the Farrows' eldest daughter as saying that, on that fateful Sunday morning, she had taken her father a cup of tea. As she handed it to her father, he allegedly said to her, "This is the last cup of tea you will bring me. You may hear I am in Northampton Gaol tonight!" To his wife, a few

Hanslope Churchyard. The gravestone of William Farrow.

minutes later, as he handed over his wages, he reputedly said, "This is the last lot of money you will have from me. This is the fatal day!" If Farrow did indeed make these remarks, in one he is not contemplating committing suicide, as he expected to be detained and taken to Northampton Gaol on a possible charge of murder. The comment to his wife can be taken as either a contemplation of murder alone, and capture and eventual hanging, or murder and suicide. Either way, Mrs. Farrow would not receive any more wages from her husband.

Squire Watts was interred a few days later in the family vault at Hanslope Church, after cremation at Golders Green. Farrow was also quietly buried at St. James' Church, but in a distant corner of the churchyard, at dark of night, with the crowd who had attended being kept at bay by a body of Police. His widow and daughters were not there. Enigmatically, Mrs. Farrow had inscribed on his gravestone the words, 'Waiting till all shall be revealed.'

For P.C. Alfred Cooper this was to be the highlight of his service with the Buckinghamshire Constabulary. He returned to the more mundane tasks confronting a rural Policeman of this era. He would be commended later on three occasions, once for effecting the arrest of a man for obtaining food and lodgings by false pretences and twice for detecting cases of fowl stealing. He was promoted Sergeant in 1913 and retired from the Buckinghamshire Constabulary in 1928.

Mrs. Watts later arranged with Buckinghamshire County Council that the part of the road where her husband had been killed be left untouched; the road to be diverted.

It was thought that she might erect some form of memorial to her husband there, but nothing came of it.[4] Perhaps she wanted to keep the place as it was when her husband died, in that late Edwardian Summer.

---

4 In 1994, a memorial plaque was placed at the scene of the murder.

(On 21st July, 2002, a short ceremony was held at the place where the Squire met his death. It was exactly 90 years to the day that he had been murdered. Several people attended who share an interest in the murder. Among those who spoke were Don Hellings, Chairman of the Hanslope and District Historical Society, Mary Bennett, Chairwoman of Hanslope Parish Council when the grove was dedicated, Jim Cowlin, the present,2002, Chairman of the Parish Council and Roger Drage, Project Co-ordinator of Milton Keynes Heritage Gateway Project, who gave a fine speech outlining the murder and its aftermath The present Police Constable for Hanslope, Police Constable 994 Mick Shaw donned a Police uniform of the period for the occasion.)

The scene of the murder as it is today.

THE GYPSY AND BIG BILL

Wraysbury - 1947

William Bissett had served the people of Staines well during his life. For over 51 years he had worked at a local linoleum firm until retiring in 1941. In the First World War he had had joined the Special Constabulary, eventually becoming a Sergeant. He had been held in high esteem, for in 1920 the Specials had presented him with a gold watch. During the interwar years he had organised the Annual Athletic Sports meetings for the Staines Police. He was also a prominent Freemason and was known throughout the community as a friendly, generous and kindly old gentleman and was affectionately called Big Bill. He had remained a bachelor all his life and lived with his sister and brother in a small house in Church St. He was also known to carry, in those days of austerity, fairly large sums of money about with him.

In his old age he enjoyed nothing more than going out of an evening, walking the short distance to the town centre and having a few drinks and a chat and strolling home. The evening of Thursday, 18th December 1947 was typical. Bissett called at Staines Conservative Club, where he had three or four gins. He left and walked along to the Cock Inn, where the landlady, Mrs. Elizabeth Cunningham, had been serving, among others, a gypsy, Joe Smith, who lived at a nearby encampment.

When Bill came in he ordered his usual drink and looked about him. The Cock Inn was a regular haunt of his and he soon noticed Joe Smith and began talking to him. They seemed to enjoy each other's company, for Mrs. Cunningham served them with several doubles thereafter.

At closing time, Bissett and Smith were the last two remaining in the public house. Bissett, who had only a few yards to walk to his home, left first, followed shortly after by Smith. However, Bill never arrived at his destination.

In the early hours of the following morning Joe Smith called at the

Church Street, Staines, as it is today.

caravan home of Ernest Smith at Wraysbury and told him that he had been in a fight with an old man that he had met in a pub. The old man had followed him to the recreation ground, where Smith had struck him and relieved him of the money he had been carrying. Smith gave the somewhat bemused Ernest ten pounds that he owed him. Ernest noticed that his caller was wearing an overcoat and trousers that appeared to be wet through, and Joe asked to borrow a pair of trousers which Ernest handed over. Ernest also observed that wrapped around Joe's head was a bloodstained scarf.

Joe now went to the nearby caravan of his father-in-law, Wisdom Davies, and he awoke the sleeping gypsy with the same astonishing story, producing a fistful of notes and slapping them down on the bed. He also showed him a watch and chain. That Joe was very drunk appeared to be confirmed to Wisdom when the young man burnt a five-pound note in the fireplace.

Joe returned to Ernest's caravan and showed him the gold watch and chain and wanted to give it to him, an offer which Ernest declined. His wife, however, handed Joe a box and, putting the watch and chain in it, he left it at the caravan.

At a more respectable hour of the morning, Ernest and Wisdom saw Joe trying to burn his scarf. "Everything's alright now," he cheerily called out. Wisdom replied sourly, "You are talking silly. I don't know what you are talking about."

Still feeling in a boastful mood, the young gypsy turned up in a the early hours of the next morning at the caravan of Belcher Lee at nearby Iver, relating the same story he had told the other two, adding that when he had left the old man he was standing up and had mumbled, "Alright," as Joe had left him. He had, he informed his fellow gypsy, taken £33 off the man and had divided it between Ernest and Wisdom, to whom he owed money. Joe stayed the remainder of that night with the surprised Belcher Lee.

In the meantime Bill Bissett's sister had reported her brother missing to the Staines Police, who commenced a search for the old man and made enquiries at the various places he had been seen. It did not take them very long to discover that Bissett had last been

The Cock Inn, Staires, as it is today.

observed in the company of Joe Smith. Accordingly, they started asking pertinent questions around the caravan site and found out some very interesting answers.

Eventually two Metropolitan Police detectives interviewed Joe Smith. "I don't know what you want with me," was his response. They asked him if he could tell them where Bill Bissett was as he was the last person to have been in the missing man's company.

"I left him at the Church," was Smith's quick reply.

"And what about the watch and chain you've been offering for sale?" was the next question.

"I didn't have a watch," Smith answered.

The two detectives briefly looked at each other. They had been doing their homework and, deciding that Smith ought to be interviewed more thoroughly, took him to Staines Police Station where he was seen by Detective Inspector Ware, who again asked him if he knew what had happened to Bill Bissett after they had been drinking in the Cock Inn.

"Yes," responded Smith. "I did drink with him and he treated me. He waited for me when they turned out and we walked down the road together. We were both drunk. He fell on me and I hit him. He fell down and I left him. I don't know what happened to him after I left him. I went home."

Smith was placed in the cells whilst the Police carried on with their investigations.

At 2am he was seen by Divisional Detective Inspector Bray and Detective Inspector Ware. "I've told him," Smith said, nodding towards Inspector Ware, "I was drinking with him." Would he care to make a written statement about it to try and help them find Bissett. Smith was agreeable, "Yes sir. I hope you find him alright."

After telling how he had met Smith in the Cock Inn and had been drinking with him until closing time, Smith's statement went on, "...the old man was waiting for me outside. The old man would not seem to go away from me and I stood talking to him for about a minute and we started walking away...down the road opposite the little pub near the church the old man fell on top of me. I think he was drunk and I had to go down and I couldn't get up for a while. The old man got up and, when I got up, I hit him in the mouth with my fist and he fell down again. Well, he never fell, he staggered against the wall and slid down on the kerb. I saw he had a watch and chain and I pulled at it. I pulled the watch out of his pocket and the chain too. Then I searched the left trousers pocket and took about thirty quid out. I had seen him put a lot of money in there when he was in the pub. I don't really know what time it was, but it was before 11 o'clock when I hit him. After I put the money and watch in my pocket, I stood and watched him get up and walk away... he swayed a bit. I think it was through the drop of beer he had in him... it must have been gone eleven when I got home...I flopped straight out on the floor and then I went to bed...I forgot to say that before I went to bed I went to Ernest Smith's caravan. I showed Ernie the old man's watch and chain. I showed him the money. He asked me where I got the watch and chain from and I told him I had knocked the old man down. He told me to sell it."

When asked about the blood on his scarf, Smith explained that he had had a nosebleed. "I went out and burnt it. It was because I was drunk. I didn't mean to hurt the old man. I hope he's alright. If I knew where he was now, I would take you there."

A thorough search was made of the various places in the caravan site by the Police, with Smith accompanying them. The coat and trousers that Smith had been wearing were found in Wisdom Davies' caravan. A freshly dug hole was also discovered in the encampment, and in it were found the jacket and trousers of Bill Bissett. Smith told the detectives where the small box containing Bissett's watch and chain were hidden. "Well, you see," he remarked rather lamely, as a detective pulled it from its hiding place, "I have looked after it because I was going to give it back."

It was almost 9am Sunday 21st December that Bill Bissett's body was found in a stream running at the back of the gypsy encampment, clothed only in his shirt and underpants. What the Police had no doubt anticipated for some time now became reality, when they realised that they were investigating a murder and not just a robbery.

D.D.I. Bray decided that he must now take a tougher stance with Joe Smith. "I don't think you've told me the whole truth about Bill Bissett," he said. Smith replied, "No. I will tell you the truth." He now made a second statement. I had £33 and the gold watch and chain and also one £5 note. I burnt this when I got home. I was drunk. That's what made me burn it. When I hit the man at the church, he staggered against the wall and that was when I took the money. He followed me... and when we got to the gateway I pushed him down just inside the gate. I didn't mean to hurt the old chap. I buried the gold watch and chain the next morning, because I was going to give it back to him. Ernie Smith and Wisdom Davies had nothing to do with it. He was quite alright when I left him. I took his trousers off because I didn't want him to go to the Police Station. He must have taken off his overcoat and jacket but I took all of his clothes away and chucked them in the brook. I did this because I didn't want him to go to the Police...he was quite alright. I buried the clothes on the Saturday in the little hole. They were in a sack."

Smith was now charged with the murder of William Bissett.

A post-mortem examination performed by Dr. Signy and Professor (later Sir) Keith Simpson revealed that at least seven fairly serious blows had been inflicted on Bissett. These were over the eyes, the mouth, the throat, the cheek and chest. Death, they concluded, was due to shock and a fractured dislocation of the neck. They also observed that there were cuts and marks on Bissett's hands and legs which appeared to have been caused after death.

As a matter of routine, Professor Simpson had the stomach contents sent to the Metropolitan Police Laboratory. A few days later came the report from Dr. Holden, the director. He had found sand particles in the stomach consistent with samples from the bed of the stream. Here was a potential timebomb, because if Bissett was already dead before being immersed in the stream as Professor Simpson had said, how had sand particles been discovered in the stomach when everyone realised that a dead body cannot swallow anything. Had Professor Simpson got it wrong? He was adamant that he had not, and he explained what had happened. Bissett had been attacked by

Smith and seriously injured. His body had been carried across the stream by some other person aiding Smith and who was also carrying Bissett's clothing. Smith had stumbled whilst crossing the stream, which accounted for the fact that his clothing was wet through. Bissett had also fallen into the stream and gulped water, before being lifted out again. Bissett's body was now concealed in the gypsy encampment and eventually placed in the stream, where it was found by the Police on the Sunday morning. Being dragged through the thicket bramble which lay between the camp and the stream would account for the post-mortem marks found on the body. On the clothes belonging to Smith, which had also been sent for examination at the Hendon Laboratory, were found traces of the same blood group as Bissett's.

The gypsy was brought before Slough Magistrates' Court for committal proceedings. (When Bissett's body had been discovered there had been a high level discussion as to which Police area it had been found in, Metropolitan or Buckinghamshire. It was decided that it was just in Buckinghamshire.)

Smith pleaded "Not guilty" and was sent for trial, appearing at Kingston Assizes in March 1948. Much was made by the defence counsel Mr. Raeburn of the time of death given by Dr. Signy and Professor Simpson and the fact that particles of sand had been found in Bissett's stomach. Smith, who gave evidence, emphatically denied murdering Bissett, although he admitted, as he had done to the Police, that he had robbed him.

The trial judge, Mr. Justice Oliver, also referred to the grains of sand found in Bissett's stomach, but directed the jury to the evidence given by the doctor and the Professor. He also made telling reference to the fact that Smith admitted taking the watch and chain, but explained that he intended handing it back to the deceased. "If he had wanted to give the watch back to the old man, he had only to walk a few hundred yards down the road. Instead he had buried it."

The jury pronounced that Smith was guilty of the murder of William Bissett but added a recommendation for mercy on account of his low mentality. When asked if he had anything to say before sentence of death was passed on him, Smith replied, "Yes, well I don't mind dying, but when you sentence me to death you sentence an innocent man."

An appeal was duly made but was dismissed. However, a few days before he was due to be executed, the Home Secretary, Mr. Chuter Ede, granted a reprieve.

'CRIME PASSIONEL!'

Chalvey - 1952

It was almost midnight on a summer's night in June and death was stalking the streets of Slough. Donald Neil Simon was searching for his wife who, he had strong reason to believe, was having an affair with another man. He intended to sort matters out when he caught up with her, and if her boyfriend was with her, so much the worse for him! The cuckolded husband had fuelled himself with drinks in several public houses in Slough and he had visited dance halls where he had thought they might be, but without success. Now he waited for them near where his wife lived and where she would eventually return, presumably escorted by her attentive lover. Simon had tried to reason with her, but he had been discarded and it had preyed on his mind. Now he was going to settle it once and for all.

As he waited he saw his wife walking along the street with her boy friend. Simon's eyes narrowed and he put his hand into his jacket pocket, clasping the handle of the revolver he had put there earlier that evening. As they approached him he pulled it out and confronted them both.

It was June 1952 and the arduous times of the previous decade or more, the years of global warfare which were then followed by the years of austerity, were now becoming a distant memory as people gradually became better off. There were plenty of jobs about and everyone had money in their pockets to spend on things other than just the necessities of life. Young people were really beginning to enjoy themselves, with fewer restraints than their parents had had to endure during the lean and hungry years of the 1930s and 1940s; even rationing was ending.

Not only were there the 'pictures' to visit, and Slough had an abundance of cinemas to choose from, including the Granada, the Ambassador, the Adelphi, the Century and the Essoldo, but there were dance halls and public houses, all tempting young persons with money to spend and wanting to let their hair down. If these did not appeal, and they wished to stay at home, there was the wireless to listen to or, if they were really up to date, then there was that novelty, the television to watch. Things were definitely looking better.

Earlier that year, George VI had died and he had seemed like a link with the past. Older people recalled the abdication crisis of 1936 and both they and younger ones remembered the war years when both the King and his Queen had moved amongst the people in their darkest hours. Now, there was to be a new Queen on the throne, and after a suitable period of mourning plans would be put in hand for her Coronation the following year. These were going to be years of hope and achievement; a new Elizabethan Age comparable to that of the first Queen Elizabeth some three hundred years before. A new age of adventure and discovery, and with it such prosperity as had never been known before.

However, there are some things that are forever unalterable. The emotions that affect us never change, including, unfortunately, those of envy, lust, greed and jealousy that can surface at any time.

Between the two Great Wars, while Britain, and indeed the world, had suffered from the effects of the Great Depression, Slough had been something of a boomtown. It had a Trading Estate with light industry, known to the local population as either 'the Dump' or 'the Depot', a legacy of the First World War which, with its numerous factories, afforded people a measure of work and relative security. Thousands flocked to the town from all over the British Isles, seeking work and alleviation from unemployment and all the miseries that went with it.

One such family was the Pearces who had moved from their Wiltshire home to Seymour Road, Chalvey. One of the daughters, Eunice Marjorie, attended the local school, but, by the time she had left, the Second World War had broken out and she went to do essential work at the Citroen factory on the Trading Estate. She had met Donald Neil Simon, then serving with the Canadian Army, and in 1943 they had married. At the close of the War, Eunice had left for

Canada, where her husband had later joined her. They had lived for a while at Fredericton, New Brunswick, but it had not worked out and in 1947 they had returned to Slough and had lived with her mother at 20 Seymour Road. Unfortunately Simon was a heavy drinker and the relationship between him and his wife began to break down. He kept his wife short of money because of his drinking, and he would make dates to take her out but then fail to keep them. Eunice would wait for her husband at home throughout the evening, only for him to return in a drunken state. Eventually, seeing that Donald was unreliable, she started to go out on her own and in this she was encouraged by her mother. If her husband managed to go with her he just stayed at the bar, drinking the evening away.

Then Eunice met Victor Brades, a 27-year-old unmarried maintenance man from St. Pauls Avenue, Slough, whom she encountered at a dance. Donald Simon at first appeared to resent the fact and attempted to meet his wife on those days when she went out. Because of his inability to remain sober, however, he was unable as usual to keep appointments. Although he appeared to have resigned himself to the fact that his wife was keeping company with another man, he became moody and resentful. When he mentioned to his wife that he would like to take her out, she would say that she was going out dancing, and having had enough of his promises by now would rebuff him. He would also come home very much the worse for drink, especially at weekends, and eventually, in November 1951, his behaviour had become so objectionable that Mrs. Pearce had turned him out of her house. He had gone to live, firstly at The George public house in the Farnham Road, then with Mr. and Mrs. Sims in Hampshire Avenue and finally in lodgings in Northampton Avenue, Slough.

The friendship between Mrs. Simon and Victor Brades developed. They started going out socially together, visiting dance halls and the like. Naturally enough this had upset Simon, and he would annoy his wife by pestering her at the High Street store, where she now worked as a supervisor. Simon had become so abusive towards his wife that the manager of the store, Louis Martinson, had spoken to him and had asked him to stop calling. Mr. Martinson later recalled that Simon had been to the store some 40 to 50 times over a 12-month period,.

"I'll kill both of them," Simon had once responded angrily.

"Don't be a fool, you'll hang," was Martinson's dismissive reply.

"I won't hang, I've been under treatment for nerves and I will plead insanity," Simon had answered.

Simon had indeed spent some time early in 1952 at Belmont Hospital for Nervous and Mental Diseases. His condition had not been helped when his wife had served divorce papers on him.

Early in 1952 there had been an incident, the outcome of which had been that he was brought before the Magistrates' Court and bound over to keep the peace.

Simon became so concerned about how the situation was developing that in February of that year he had called on Brades' mother and informed her that her son was going out with his wife. He asked her to speak to Brades about it. Simon told her that he did not want her to think that her son was responsible for the separation, as he realised that it was his own fault through drinking. He added that he had been to see a priest about this problem and hoped to get treatment. He also told her, "I still love my wife and I shall never let her divorce me."

It was whilst he was staying at the Hampshire Avenue address, that Mr. Sims, the landlord, saw Simon with a revolver in his bedroom. "You can't keep that, Don," Sims had remarked. Simon had handed the gun and some rounds of ammunition to his landlord for safekeeping. When he had moved to the Northampton Avenue address, Simon had called on Mr. Sims and had asked for the revolver. Sims informed him that he could not have it.

"It belongs to my brother and it is licensed," Simon had argued. Sims, however, was firm and would not entrust the gun to him.

The next day, Sims had arrived home to find that his wife was handing over the weapon to Simon. This time Sims' resolve was not so strong. "I let it go," he said later.

On the evening of Saturday, 21st June, Simon visited his mother in law. He asked her if Eunice was still going out with Brades. Mrs.

Pearce had replied that as far as she knew she was. Simon thought this over for a while, then left the house.

He went to the Good Companions public house and then the Palais de Dance but failed to find Eunice. He called at the Three Tuns public house on the Bath Road and The Flags in Chalvey, almost opposite Seymour Road. By the time he left he was well 'liquored-up.'

Simon then walked the few yards to the shop on the corner of Church Street and Seymour Road and, hiding in the doorway, he waited for Eunice to return. He heard her coming along the road with Brades and he stepped out to confront them. Taking the gun from his pocket, Simon pointed it at them, and kept firing it until it was empty. Both Brades and Eunice fell to the ground, mortally wounded.

Simon threw away the gun and knelt down beside his wife, holding her in his arms and kissing her.

Several people in the houses nearby had heard the sound of shooting and rushed outside to see the pathetic scene. Mrs. Pearce also ran to the corner of the road, where she saw her daughter dying in the street, her estranged husband weeping. As she nervously approached, Simon looked up and on seeing her cried out, "Mum, Mum, what have I done?"

A Mr. Broad, who was in the living room of his house when he heard the shots rushed out and saw Simon cradling his wife. "I have shot my wife by Christ! I have shot my wife!" he howled.

As Mr. Broad looked on at the husband and wife on the ground Eunice Simon moaned, "Why did you do it Don?"

The Police were summoned and Inspector Sidney MacBrien and Detective Sergeant, later Chief Superintendent Leslie Strong were among the first on the scene. Simon said to them matter of factly, "Here I am. I'm the man. I shot them!"

The Police Inspector enquired where the gun was that he had used and Simon replied," I slung it over there," and pointed towards the ground by the shop.

Detective Sergeant Strong then quietly asked him what had led up to this and Simon poured out the story of his life with Eunice, his drunken bouts, the arguments between them, during one of which he had ripped her dress. On another occasion whilst in the bar of a town centre public house, he continued, "I called her something I would not like to repeat."

Other Police had by now arrived and Simon was placed under arrest in a Police car, sitting next to Detective Constable, later Detective Chief Inspector, Leslie Bishop.

Simon asked the detective, "Is she dead?"

"I do not know," D.C.Bishop replied.

Simon looked at Brades, "They don't seem to be doing much for him. He's the boyfriend. I shot him." There was a pause, and then as if Simon felt the need to confide in someone, he added, "This has been going on for nearly three years. I knew she was meeting him." Simon paused again. "Thank God there's no children," he sighed.

"She was standing there," Simon indicated to the detective. "Things came to a climax. I took the gun from my pocket. I fired at her twice. I think I hit her in the arm. I then shot him. It must have been five rounds, can't remember."

Referring to how he had waited for them in the entrance to the shop, Simon related, "I pulled out the ice cream box and stood behind it. ...Somehow I don't feel like crying....I feel better now I've told you. You will find out how she is for me?"

He was then conveyed to Slough Police Station where he was seen again by Detective Sergeant Strong. Simon told the softly spoken detective that when he had started shooting, Eunice had fallen first. "...Vic stepped forward to try and stop me but it was too late and he had it. I lay down on the ground beside her for about ten minutes."

The detective listened patiently, as Simon told him about events leading up to the murder, and wrote down what he had to say.

"I came home one night late and said to my missus, ' I would like to go to a dance with you,' and she said, 'No you can't go, this is my night out.' I grabbed her by the shoulder and ripped her dress. There was another night when I told her I should come down to The Crown (a public house in Slough town centre). I said I did not want to see anyone mauling her about. In the bar I smashed a glass in her hand. From that night it has been one big merry go round."

Detective Sergeant Leslie Strong.

Simon further related how one evening he had returned to his mother-in-law's home after one of his drinking bouts and had passed some vile remarks. He had also, on previous occasions, threatened his wife. Once he had told her to get out of the marital bed and go and sleep with her mother or else he would kick her downstairs. He said how he had left work at Langley and had walked to Marks and Spencer, where his wife worked, to see her as she left. Later he had called at the house of a friend with whom he had left a revolver and said that he now wanted it returned to him. At first his friend had refused, but then he had relented and handed the weapon over to him.

Simon had then visited a dance hall looking for his wife but had failed to see her and had therefore waited in Seymour Road for her. He had seen Eunice and Brades turn into the road and he had confronted them saying, "At last I've caught up with you! Where are you going?"

Eunice had replied, "Home."

"Well none of us are going home tonight!" Simon said emphatically and had begun shooting. "I think she was hit first and Vic tried to stop me and he seemed to get it."

Simon was charged with the murder of Victor Brades and later, when his wife died in hospital, he was further charged with her murder and duly appeared before the Slough Magistrates.

Simon intimated through his solicitor that he would be pleading, 'Not guilty' and was committed to the Assizes.

It was at Birmingham Assizes that the case was set for hearing and the Prosecuting Counsel, Mr. C.N. Shawcross outlined the case for the jury. "It was, " he began, "a crime of passion," adding that Mrs. Simon and Brades were both shot in Seymour Road, Chalvey, although they, the jury, were not directly concerned with Brades' death. (How they would be able to ignore it, however, would be a problem.)

Witnesses stepped up into the box to testify as to the background and the events that had taken place that fatal Saturday night. It was

Simon was later arrested at Seymour Road and taken to Slough police station where, in the early hours of Sunday, Detective-sergeant Leslie Strong charged him with the murder of Victor Brades. On Monday morning he was charged with the murder of his wife. He made statements in answer to both charges.

The Chairman (Mr. R. R. Purser) said that legal aid would be granted.

In court Simon wore a brown suit, white shirt, and tartan tie. Later he returned to court and sat trembling between two police officers during the opening of the inquest on his wife and Victor Brades. The proceedings were conducted by the Deputy South Bucks Coroner, Mr. E. Woodward.

Evidence of identification was given by Fred Desmond Kendall, also of Seymour Road, who said that Mrs. Simon was his sister-in-law, and by Geoffrey Brades, Baylis Road, Slough, who said he was a brother of Victor Brades. The proceedings were adjourned to a date to be arranged.

AT MONTEM SCHOOL

Mrs. Simon was the fourth daughter of nine (four sons and five daughters) and lived at her mother's home. She was born at Melksham, Wilts, and moved with her family to Slough after the death of her father, Mr. John Herbert Pearce, 17 years ago.

She was, for several years, a

Victor Brades

pupil at Montem School. Later she went to work at the Citroen plant at Slough, and worked in the depot assembling there throughout the war.

Early in the war she met Simon at Slough Community Centre. He was then serving with the Canadian forces and stationed at Aldershot. They were married at the Hampshire Avenue Methodist Church, Slough, in November 1943.

In 1945, Mrs. Simon sailed to Canada in a war-brides' liner. She and her husband made their home at Fredricton, in the province of New Brunswick, until 1947, when Mrs. Simon was advised to return home for health reasons. She and her husband then returned to Slough and lived in Seymour Road.

NO CHILDREN

Since her return to England, Mrs. Simon had been working at the Slough branch of Marks and Spencer Ltd. She had been training for duties as a supervisor there. She had no children.

Mrs. Simon was one of a family

Donald Simon

of seven. Three of her four sisters

Eunice Simon

mechanic, volunteering for service at the age of 17. Before that he had served in the Home Guard. His five years' service in the Fleet Air Arm took him to many parts of the world.

After the former war in the aircraft carrier "Nabob". He was demobilised in 1946. For the last five years he had been employed as a maintenance carpenter at Hammersmith. He was a member of the Slough R.E.M.E. Territorial branch.

His father was a member of the Royal Flying Corps during the Great War and his mother was one of the first members of the Women's Auxiliary Corps, established in 1917. Mrs. Brades served in France as a cook.

Victor Brades was unmarried. He was the eldest of three brothers. Following a service at St. Paul's Church, Slough, this (Friday) morning, he will be buried in the Borough cemetery.

Site Sought For Scout Hut

Old Windsor Parish Council on Tuesday considered a letter from Sir Henry Abel-Smith asking if the Council could provide land on which to build a Scout hut. He understood the Council might be willing to give up some allotment ground.

The Council decided to tell Sir Henry Abel-Smith that they did not wish to relinquish any more allotment ground, and to refer him to the County Planning Officer.

MUSIC RECITAL

A music recital will be given at Eton Parish Church on 3rd July, at 8 p.m., in aid of the funds of Eton Wick Church.

Victor Brades, Eunice Simon and Donald Simon.

also mentioned that the defendant had attended Belmont Park hospital

Dr. David Montague Jackson, Registrar at Upton Hospital, Slough stated that on arrival at hospital Mrs. Simon had given one or two breaths after which there was no sign of life. Various forms of artificial respiration had been tried but to no avail and she had died shortly after admission.

Professor, later Sir, Keith Simpson, the Home Office pathologist, said in evidence that when he had conducted a post-mortem on the body of Eunice Simon he had recovered two .38 bullets. One had passed through her spine, and death was due to shock and internal bleeding caused by the wounds to her arm and chest. Two further bullets had been found in Brades' body, including one that had travelled through his heart and lung.

When the defence presented their case they heard, first of all, Dr.Ernst Jacobi, the senior medical officer at Birmingham Mental Hospital. He said that an electric test he carried out on Simon revealed that he had abnormalities, which would make it more difficult for him to control himself than a normal person. The case history of the defendant when he entered Belmont Hospital was a typical history," he stated, " of psychopathic personality."

Dr. John Humphrey, the Principal Medical Officer at Birmingham Prison, arrived at the conclusion that although Simon was a neurotic type he had never, at any time, suffered from any disease of the mind which would prevent him from knowing that what he was doing was wrong.

When the Medical Officer of Shrewsbury Prison, Dr. A.V. Mackenzie, was asked by Mr. Richard O'Sullivan, defending, "Assume a man is in love with his wife and assume that he has put himself in a hospital for nervous diseases in order to cure himself and assume that while he is there he gets a petition for divorce served upon him. Would that greatly disturb him?"

Dr. Mackenzie replied, " I certainly agree. It would disturb him."

Despite all the medical evidence produced by the defence, however, the jury found Simon guilty and the judge, Mr. Justice Jones, duly sentenced him to death.

Mr. O'Sullivan took the case to the Court of Criminal Appeal and argued his case in front of the Lord Chief Justice, Lord Goddard, flanked by Mr. Justice Finnemore and Mr. Justice McNair. Mr. O'Sullivan said that his main ground of appeal was that there was evidence of insanity that should have been put to the jury, inasmuch as Simon might not have known at the time that what he did was wrong. The defence set out that Simon did not realise that what he was doing was unlawful killing. The jury at the trial had been misdirected and that a true verdict would have been one of manslaughter.

Lord Goddard, in giving judgement, stated that the Court of Criminal Appeal could not see how, in the circumstances, the verdict could be reduced to manslaughter. There was no defence other than the usual one of insanity, and there was no evidence of insanity.

"To shoot two people," the Lord Chief Justice summed up, " I can see no evidence of insanity at all. We are asked to say that he was a psychopathic personality but no doctor said he was insane." The appeal was dismissed. (Offenders or their counsel who cited insanity as a means of avoiding the ultimate penalty did not apparently sway Lord Goddard. He had made abundantly clear his views on such claims in his evidence before the Royal Commission on Capital Punishment some years before.)

The only hope now for Simon lay in a recommendation for a reprieve by the Home Secretary and when that was not forthcoming his fate was sealed. At eight o'clock on the morning of Thursday, 23rd October 1952, Donald Simon was executed at Shrewsbury Prison.

JUST ANOTHER
DOMESTIC DISPUTE!

High Wycombe - 1958

Edna May Roberts was a loser in love. She had married one Harry Collins just before the outbreak of the Second World War, and had borne him a daughter. Harry had joined the Army when war had broken out and had been posted to Singapore. He was captured when that citadel capitulated in 1942 and he became a prisoner of war of the Japanese. He never returned, and at the cessation of hostilities was reported as, 'Missing, presumed dead.'

Edna, meantime, was determined that life should not pass her by just because her husband was overseas during the war years, and she became friendly with some of the American Servicemen who were stationed around the town of High Wycombe where she lived. She also frequented public houses in the town and went to the pictures.

After the conclusion of the Second World War, and after being notified of her husband's presumed death, she met a Merchant Seaman by the name of Ron Roberts, and when he was not at sea she went out with him. The romance blossomed and marriage appeared to be on the cards.

There was, however, something that should have acted like a warning beacon to Edna. Roberts could be quite violent towards her. On one occasion he had met her as she came out of Woolworth's, where she was then working. He had demanded money from her, struck her and then snatched her handbag, which contained £20, which was a fair sum of money in those years of austerity just after the Second World War.

The violence shown by Roberts towards her had already cost her one job. She had been working in a greengrocer's in High Wycombe, but when she consistently arrived at work with black eyes, and bruises on her arms and forehead, the shop manager informed her that her services were no longer required. He told her that, "It did not look right...being in the shop with those bruises." Edna replied that Roberts had knocked her about. The manager's opinion was that she should leave him.

When Edna's brother, who was serving abroad in the Army at the time, heard of this, he wrote to his sister, and he also told her to stop seeing Roberts. Edna of course should have taken her younger brother's advice, but she allowed her heart to rule her head and the courtship continued.

The trouble was that, when Roberts had consumed alcohol, he turned nasty and would turn up at 17, Wendover Street, High Wycombe, her parents' address, and where Edna was living at the time. He would be abusive to both her and to her parents. He would use foul language, and, if left outside the house, he would throw stones at the windows. This was all very upsetting to those inside No. 17, but it provided good theatre to the neighbours, of course.

Despite all this, Edna married Ronald Roberts around 1950. They settled in High Wycombe and she bore him two children, a girl and a boy. When Edna's father died a few years later, the Roberts family moved in with her mother at Wendover Street.

Matters had not improved with the marriage and there were constant rows and worse between them, so much so that Edna's mother could no longer put up with the disturbances and left to live with her son and his wife. Edna's daughter, by her first marriage, also moved out and sought lodgings elsewhere.

Edna often appeared in the town with black eyes and bruising, and it therefore came as no surprise that she decided that she would leave her violent husband, take the children with her, and seek maintenance through the court.

It was during this period of separation that Edna met a man and went out with him on one or two occasions. After a while Edna agreed to return to her husband. It was to be a fatal decision.

On the morning of Sunday, 14th September 1958, a woman, who lived in a house at the rear of Wendover Street, looked over the garden and saw Edna hanging out the washing on a clothesline. That afternoon she noticed the two children playing by the side of the house. Later, that evening she happened to glance over again at 17, Wendover Street and observed that the house was in darkness, something she thought was unusual, as Mr. and Mrs. Roberts, to her knowledge, usually kept late hours. Dismissing the thought, she pulled her curtains to and settled down for the night.

On the morning of Monday, 15th September, Inspector Norman Priestley was on duty at the Police Station in High Wycombe, when he was informed that a man wished to see him, in his capacity as a senior Police Officer.

The Inspector saw that the man, whose name had been given as Ronald Roberts, was accompanied by two young children and Inspector Priestley asked him what was so important that he could not tell the other Police Officers his business.

"My wife is dead," Roberts replied.

Inspector Priestley was a little puzzled, for if it was just a sudden death that the man wished to report, that could be dealt with by any Constable acting as a Coroner's Officer. "How did she die?" he queried.

"We had a row last night and she cut my arm," Roberts responded and held out his right arm and showed the Policeman several severe cuts to his fingers. Not unnaturally the Inspector winced slightly as he saw the injuries.

Inspector Priestley now became very interested in this matter, which appeared to be taking on a sinister appearance. "How did she die?" he repeated.

"I don't know," Roberts replied. "She's on the bed." Adding as an afterthought, "What's going to happen to the children?"

Placing the man in the custody of a Policeman and ensuring that the two young, bewildered children were looked after, Inspector Priestley conferred with Superintendent George Healey, the officer in charge of High Wycombe Division of the Buckinghamshire Constabulary, and these two Officers, with Detective Sergeant Barratt, went to 17, Wendover Street.

The three Policemen trooped upstairs to a back bedroom where

The house where Edna May Roberts was murdered.

they discovered the corpse of a woman lying on a bed covered by a blanket.

Carefully, Inspector Priestley drew back the blanket and perceived that the partly clothed body was lying on its back, with a pillow covering the nose and mouth and part of the face. As he looked closer the Police Officer could discern several stab wounds around the lower neck, whilst the victim's right eye was swollen and blackened. There was also, as the Inspector looked carefully around, a considerable amount of blood on the pillows and bedding.

A Police Surgeon was summoned to the scene to comply with the law and state that Edna Roberts was actually dead.

On his return to High Wycombe Police Station, Inspector Priestley re-interviewed Roberts. He told him that he had been to his address and had seen the body of his wife. He also stated that he had seen the stab wounds that had been inflicted upon her. Now he wanted to know just what had transpired.

"We've had one or two rows and I suspected her of having an affair with the lodger," was the reply. "When I came home late one night, I heard the patter of feet. I suspected something was going on with the lodger. I turned him out last Thursday." Roberts paused, then resumed his narrative. "Yesterday, I was lying on the bed and she came up with a knife in her hand. She was raving and tried to slash me. I hit her eye and gave her a black eye. When I came back, she still had the knife and in trying to take it away I cut my hand. Then I forget what happened. There was a lot of blood about and I was in a daze at this stage."

Roberts was charged with the murder of his wife, to which he responded, "I didn't murder her, I loved her too much." He was brought before the Magistrates' Court and remanded in custody.

A few days later, Inspector Priestley was a little surprised when he received a telephone call from the Chief Prison Officer at Oxford saying that Roberts wanted to see him.

When he visited him at the gaol, Roberts said that he wanted to add something to what he had already told the Police. As they had treated him fairly he wished to tell them that after killing his wife he

64

had attempted to gas himself and the two children. When he had disclosed this information to the Police Inspector, Roberts seemed relieved and commented, "Now I have told you all that, I think I shall sleep tonight."

A few weeks later, at Leicestershire Assizes, Ronald Roberts pleaded guilty to the charge of murder and was sentenced to life imprisonment.

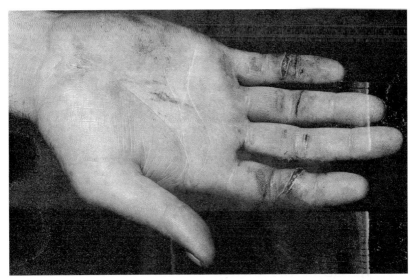

The hand of a killer!

THE MURDER OF
THE GOOD DOCTOR

Amersham - 1966

When the six-year-old son of Tony Dale fell over and bumped his head one Saturday afternoon in early November 1966, Tony asked his local G.P. to call and see the boy to ensure that he was alright. In the event, Dr. Helen Davidson, from the same practice although not the Dale family's regular doctor, visited the household instead. She looked at the boy, and such was her concern for his welfare that she re-attended the next day. Little did Tony Dale realise that not only would he see the doctor a few days later under vastly different and calamitous circumstances, but also that Dr. Davidson would, to a certain extent, follow him for the rest of his career and then even after he retired. For Tony Dale was a Detective Sergeant in the Buckinghamshire Constabulary and the next time he saw the friendly doctor, after she had attended his son, was when he stared down at her dreadfully battered body.

To the people of Amersham, Dr. Helen Davidson was a popular figure, ministering tirelessly to their ailments. She had arrived in the town just after the end of the Second World War. In 1961, she had married a man several years older than herself, retired bank official Herbert Baker. She was his second wife, his first having died.

Helen Davidson retained her maiden name for use in her professional capacity.

On Wednesday, 9th November 1966, at approximately 1.35pm, Mr. Baker left the house the couple occupied in Chesham Bois. His wife must have left shortly after, because at 2.30pm she visited two patients in Amersham and had then called at the Express Dairy and purchased a bottle of milk. For an hour there were no more sightings of her, until she was seen driving up nearby Gore Hill. Whether

Dr. Helen Davidson.

anything significant or even sinister occurred during that time was never discovered. In fact she probably spent the time perfectly innocently, either at home or elsewhere in the vicinity

When Mr. Baker returned home that afternoon, Helen was not there. He also noted that her car was not in its usual place, and his wife's dog, a wirehaired fox terrier named Fancy, was also absent. He assumed that she had taken advantage of a relatively free afternoon to go bird watching in one of the several woods that abound in this area of the Chiltern Hills. However, as darkness fell and his wife had still not returned home, Mr. Baker became more and more concerned for her well being. Perturbed by her continued absence, he mentioned the fact to some neighbours, who carried out an immediate search of the area. When they could not find her and she had still not come home, the Police were notified.

After taking sufficient details to complete a 'missing person' report, the Police made a more extensive search of the locality. A description of the doctor's car, a Hillman saloon, was given to the night shift as they reported for duty, and in the early hours of the next morning it was seen, parked and unattended, in a lay-by just off the Amersham to Beaconsfield road at Hodgemoor Wood. Ominously, it looked just as it must have been when Dr. Davidson had left it some hours before. Her handbag and binocular case were seen to be inside the vehicle, but of the doctor and her dog there was no sign. Darkness precluded a more thorough search of the area and it was not until first light that it could be undertaken. Fears for the doctor's safety were uppermost in the minds of many of those present.

The large number of Policemen taking part was augmented by Gurkha and British soldiers from Beaconsfield. An inch by inch search of the wood now took place. Even allowing for the fact that it was Autumn and the wood was not so densely covered by foliage as it would have been earlier in the year, it was a painstaking and frustrating job, and it was not until the afternoon that a Police Cadet, accompanied by a soldier, found the body of Dr. Davidson lying in a quiet secluded part of the wood.

She had been savagely beaten, and the young soldier, after

Police find the body of Dr Davidson, guarded by her dog, Fancy.

summoning the senior Police Officer to the scene, was understandably violently sick. It was a sight that few Policemen, hardened as they might be to terrible sights, would ever wish to see again during their service. For not only had the doctor's skull been fractured, but her assailant had jumped on her until her head was buried several inches into the earth.

At the same time there was an additional air of pathos added to the scene that greeted the search party's eyes, when they noticed that Fancy was lying between the doctor's legs, as if waiting patiently for her to arise. The faithful dog was unaware of the tragedy that had befallen her mistress.

Mindful of the fact that they were dealing with a major murder investigation, the Chief Constable of Buckinghamshire, Brigadier John Norman Cheney, sent an urgent message to the Commissioner of the Metropolitan Police requesting that he send a senior detective to co-ordinate the hunt for the killer. Brigadier Cheney had himself visited the scene and commented to a journalist, "I only wish the Home Secretary could have seen how she was murdered by some devil. I think he would have changed his mind about hanging. Devils like this must be punished." It must be remembered that capital punishment had recently been abolished by Parliament.

When Detective Sergeant Dale viewed the body of the doctor who had so recently attended his young son, he remarked that his first impression was that it appeared that the doctor had no head, so appalling were her injuries. "She was lying face upwards and her face was absolutely covered in blood, which was black by the time we all came on the scene." He continued, "It looked as if once she was on the ground, her killer had repeatedly stamped on her head so that the back of her head had been driven into the soil." As for Fancy, the Detective Sergeant added, "She just looked at us. She stayed without moving for an hour or two while we worked round her. She just followed us with her eyes. Then eventually somebody took her away to the Police Station to feed her. She couldn't have had anything to eat or drink for twenty four hours."

In response to the Chief Constable's application, Detective

Det. Sergt. Tony Dale.

Superintendent Jack Williams of Scotland Yard was despatched to aid his country colleagues. On his arrival, he was taken to see the body of the doctor in situ. The corpse was then removed to the mortuary at Amersham Hospital for a post-mortem examination to be carried out. A task performed by Dr. David Bowen, senior lecturer in forensic medicine at Charing Cross Hospital.

He would state later at the Inquest that the only injuries to the doctor were to her head. Her death, he would say, must have been instantaneous and caused by a haemorrhage due to a fractured skull. Dr. Bowen would also mention that there was a slight bruise or scorch mark on Dr. Davidson's neck which he believed was caused by pressure from the strap of her binoculars when they had been pressed into the ground during the attack. He would add that she had been dead for approximately twenty-four hours when she had been found.

In the meantime, however, extensive enquiries were made to trace the murderer, and so thorough and extensive were these that eventually 70 people were traced and interviewed who had been in Hodgemoor Wood around the time that Dr. Davidson had been murdered. Even some couples, who had been conducting clandestine affairs, were interviewed. Whatever they had to tell the Police Officers, their reasons for being in the wood at that particular time remained confidential, for these were matters of little concern to the detectives investigating such an atrocious killing. None of those seen could come up with the really vital clue that would lead the Police to the murderer.

Of course, the usual probing but discreet enquiries were made into the doctor's background, but these provided nothing tangible, as Dr. Davidson led a blameless life devoted to the care of others. It was suggested that perhaps she had arranged to meet someone in the wood, but nothing ever came of that enquiry. It emerged that, as a keen ornithologist, the doctor was interested not only in the sightings of rare birds, but also in the habits of native species, and there was nothing sinister in her going to Hodgemoor Wood late on an Autumn evening.

There appeared one somewhat promising lead, when someone mentioned seeing a Vauxhall Viva saloon with the registration number F.L.P. or something similar, but despite massive enquiries it proved impossible to trace. (These were the days before the centralised and computerised Driver and Vehicle Licensing Authority.)

When Detective Superintendent Williams was asked who he thought might be the person responsible, he replied that in his opinion it was most likely to be someone local who might have difficulty keeping the murder to himself, and he made an appeal to the public that anyone who might have suspicions about any person should contact the Police.

The really perplexing thing about the murder appeared to be the motive behind it. Robbery was ruled out, as no attempt had been made to remove Dr. Davidson's jewellery or binoculars. Neither was there evidence of a sexual attack, and if her killer was someone seeking revenge for some reason or other, the Police failed to discover anyone with even the remotest reason.

Perhaps the doctor had witnessed something that she had not been meant to see and that person had determined that she should not live to relate the incident to anyone else. A couple conducting an illicit affair, and possibly believing that the doctor had been spying on them? A theory that would have to be looked into, obviously, but the persons involved would have to have been pretty desperate to kill an innocent witness.

Or could it have been someone who had suddenly jumped out on the doctor and had indecently exposed himself? For these pests, or 'flashers' as they are known to the Police, just wait for a single female out walking in an isolated part of the countryside. Then, possibly realising that Dr. Davidson had recognised him, this 'flasher' had callously killed her. After all, the ferocious attack made on the doctor's head could be construed as an attempt to put her eyes out. There is, or was, a belief that the eyes of a victim recorded the last image ever seen and that this could somehow be retrieved.

If it had been someone the doctor knew, could she not have reasoned with him? She had done it before, as Tony Dale recalled later that she was used to dealing with difficult people and recounted that, whilst he had been in the waiting room of her surgery one day, he had heard a patient of the doctor shouting at her. Dr. Davidson had, by keeping very calm, managed to control the situation. But, of course, reasoned argument does not always win the day.

The one thing the Police could be certain of was that it had been a chance encounter, as the piece of wood that had been used to batter the doctor had obviously been picked up either at or near the scene. The murder weapon had not been taken to where it had been used. Therefore, the Police reasoned, the murder had not been pre-planned.

Among the first suspects were the men working at a small charcoal producing concern which was operating in the wood, but after they had been interviewed they were eliminated. The search then widened to include Dr. Davidson's patients, but nothing could be proved against any of them.

All possible scenarios were of course investigated but, with no really useful information coming in, the investigation of necessity began to wind down.

Detective Superintendent Williams returned to the 'Yard' and Detective Inspector Ernest Lund of the Buckinghamshire Constabulary was left in charge to follow up any further enquiries. In January of 1968, this slim, quietly spoken, pipe smoking detective retired, and it seemed as though the file on the murder would be closed.

However, each year, as the anniversary of the slaying came round, the local press would send a reporter to interview Detective Sergeant Dale, who would obligingly take them to the murder scene in order that a photograph could be taken and a story be published, with a view, hopefully, to jogging someone's memory. Or perhaps persuade someone to come forward with the information that would at last lead to the enquiry being reopened and possibly to a solution.

Det. Insp. Ernest Lund.

Occasionally, a national newspaper would print an article on the slaying and Sergeant Dale would patiently go over the whole matter again, but seldom would anything come of it, and Tony Dale would return to the day to day inquiries into criminal activity on his 'patch'.

Some six years after the murder, when it had been raised once more, Inspector John Pearson of Amersham heard via a source that there was a lady who used to walk her dogs through Hodgemoor Woods. It was still a popular place for clandestine meetings. She indicated that she had been stalked by a man on several occasions, but then one time she had managed to turn the tables on him and had tracked him back to the lay-by on the main road which runs by the woods. She had not only got a good look at the man but had taken details of the lorry in which he drove away from the area. The Inspector had the man's driving documents discreetly checked, and mentioned the matter to his officers. It transpired that they knew of him and his lorry, as they had checked it in various isolated spots where courting couples went, even during the daylight hours. He was strongly suspected of being a 'peeper', one of those persons who get a thrill out of watching courting couples perform their rituals. He had been seen on occasions well off his route. Furthermore, he had been a patient of Dr. Davidson! Inspector Pearson and Sergeant Dale consulted the case file. They found that this man had come 'into the frame', but, when he had said that his route had not taken him past the murder site, the suspicion appeared not to have been pursued. The Police who covered the ground knew about his deviations, but nobody on the murder team had sought their local knowledge. As Inspector Pearson, now retired, says, "The alibi he gave was flawed, but nobody spotted it."

Then there was the information received from a lady who had contacted the Murder Incident Room. She was a cultured lady, as the ex Inspector recalls, and, after apologising for contacting the Police as she thought she might be wasting their time, she felt she was bound to tell them of her experience. She lived in the West Country and seemed to know more about the case than appeared in the newspapers. She related to one of the team a dream she had had. She felt that Dr. Davidson's spirit had made contact with her, being on the same intellectual level as her. In the dream she described the area where the murder had taken place. But then she added that she had 'seen' a man running from the place of the murder to a lay-by. She described the man, and the two Police Officers realised that the description fitted the lorry driver! The coincidence seemed remarkable. The lorry driver had not at the time been interviewed on this basis, however well meaning the lady was who had taken the trouble to telephone the Incident Room. The two Policemen, Inspector Pearson and Sergeant Dale, interviewed the man, and after some preliminary questioning it was put to him that he was the murderer, which he denied, although he did admit to doing a bit of 'peeping'. The two Police Officers detected some sort of subdued, frustrated anger in the man's make-up, but that was all. All they had to go on was a dream and they both decided that the case could not be re-opened on that basis.

Then there was the strange episode of the hanging man! He committed suicide in one of the nearby villages and left a note saying that he had committed the murder, but he had never been a suspect and was not even a patient of Dr. Davidson.

Another set of circumstances then presented themselves to the Police. Just after the doctor had been murdered, a local man, who shall be called for the sake of this narrative, Mr. A., had emigrated to Australia. It appeared that this was coincidental, as the emigration had been planned prior to the killing. Indeed the man later admitted that he might even have approached the doctor for a reference for his application to the Australian authorities. Whilst living in that country he came to the notice of the Police when he beat to death two dogs owned by his wife. Then he had advertised in an Australian newspaper for people to accompany him on an 'intergalactic flying saucer', stating that he was looking for a better way of life.

It was shortly after this episode that he returned to this country to live in Amersham.

In 1979, he was stopped by the Police for a motoring offence and upbraided the Officer who had detained him, saying that they should be concentrating on discovering the killer of the doctor, not persecuting him as a motorist. Now, had this remark been made in 1966, it might have been dismissed as the ranting of an aggrieved member of the public, thinking that the Police had other, more important things to do than harassing the motorist. But this was thirteen years after the crime!

Shortly afterwards, an old man was violently attacked, being struck about the head with an iron bar. As he was taken to hospital, he kept muttering the name of Dr. Davidson. Mr. A. was arrested for this crime, although he was eventually charged with a somewhat lesser offence.

Eighteen months later, Detective Chief Inspector Norman Robson, who was now stationed at Amersham, decided to re-open the case and had Mr. A. arrested and brought to the Police Station. There he was interrogated for almost 48 hours about his possible involvement in the Hodgemoor Wood murder. He was eventually released without charge.

He was however traced and interviewed by Peter Game of the News of the World and admitted to the journalist that he had a poor memory about the time Dr. Davidson had been murdered. "It's a bit of blank period," he said, adding, "I am a medium, and fate will have its way. I denied killing the woman and I am free for the moment, but they might want to see me again." Referring to the incidents when he had been stopped by the Police and arrested for the attack on the old man, he confided to Peter Game, "All that points to me. I was one of Dr. Davidson's patients. She was a wonderful woman, everyone loved her. She was very good to me. I am the man stopped for the alleged driving offence and told detectives to find her killer. But the facts which pinpoint me could relate to lots of other people. I am in contact with spirits on another plane. I know things are going to happen. I knew some time ago I was going to be arrested, but even so it came as a bit of a surprise. I told the Police I didn't know who the killer was. I have arranged to communicate with them through my special powers...I know that somewhere in Amersham the killer is on the loose but I can't commit myself to saying any more than that..." The News of the World ran the article and offered £100,000 for information leading to the arrest and conviction of the murderer, but no more was heard.

So the murder remains unsolved, and now, over thirty years afterwards, is likely to remain so, despite the intense Police activities which have taken place since the commission of the crime.

"I THUMPED HIM!
DON'T ASK ME WHY!"

Bledlow Ridge - 1967

It must be the aspiration of many Police Officers, from when they first join the Police and right through their service, to actually apprehend a murderer! In the late 20th and early 21st centuries, when all we ever seem to hear or read about are the number of murders that have been or are being committed, the general public must think that all the Police seem to do is to go around arresting murderers.

Mention that to a Policeman and he will probably smile indulgently and reply that actually very few Policemen, even C.I.D. officers, come across a murderer, let alone arrest one, either at the scene of the crime or shortly after he or she has committed their vile act.

One of those very few Policemen who can actually boast of having arrested a murderer in, virtually, 'flagrante delicto' is Steuart Ayres, now a retired Inspector of the Thames Valley Police. In the late 1960s he was the village Constable for Bledlow Ridge. He had joined the Buckinghamshire Constabulary in 1961 and after initial training had been sent to High Wycombe. In 1964 he had been posted to Bledlow Ridge, where the pace of life was not nearly so hectic as being a Policeman in a large town could be. Here in a village the local Constable can truly integrate with his 'parishioners'. People looked up to 'their Policeman', and they could rely upon him to look after them.

He would be able to devote more time to Police matters. He could also patrol his 'patch' and be a highly visible representative of the Buckinghamshire, and thereby the British, Police.

Actually, the locality surrounding High Wycombe was the setting for more than its fair share of crimes and it was because of this that P.C. Ayres realised what many other Policemen could only dream of.

In 1967, George Castle lived with his wife and two young children in the village. They had lived at their present address for two years, prior to which they had lived with an 84-year-old widower called Fred Brooks. The Castles had shared two rooms in the house, 1, Church Cottages, Church Lane, Bledlow Ridge, otherwise known as Council Cottages. They had not got on too well with their 'landlord', whose personal habits were rather off-putting, and George Castle, his wife and Brooks, had rowed over various household matters. All in all, the Castles were quite pleased to have left and found a house all to themselves.

Fred Brooks had lived at Bledlow Ridge since the 1930s, with his wife. They were a childless couple and Mrs. Brooks had died in the early 1950s. Fred always carried a large amount of cash about with him. He had been warned that he should bank it, but he usually shrugged off the friendly advice.

On the evening of Saturday, 5th August, George Castle had finished work and had returned home. He was irritable that evening; he tended to suffer from bad headaches, and after having his tea he mowed the lawn. Mrs. Castle's aunt called round and they had a glass of sherry each. When she had left, George decided to take his family out for a drink and he drove his wife and children over to Saunderton. After having a couple of lager and limes George drove the family back to their house and the children were put to bed. George's irritability was no better, and when his wife had gone to bed he told her that he was going out for another drink. Mrs. Castle expected him back shortly.

A few minutes later, Edward Marsden, who also lived in the village, decided that he would take a stroll out in the summer night. He was walking around his garden when he heard the sound of footsteps on his driveway. At first he thought it was his son returning home and called out to him. There was no reply, and Mr. Marsden went back to his house to fetch a torch. As he came back out to the garden he could see that his son, who had come home in his car, was now talking to someone.

When he was asked what he was doing in the driveway, all the man could say was, "I've done no harm. I've been out for a walk, found it was a house at the end and I've come back."

Mr. Marsden shone his torch over the man but did not recognise him. He noted, however, that he was wearing, amongst other clothing, a fawn mackintosh, and although he kept one hand in a pocket, on the other hand he had on a glove. Inappropriate clothing for a summer night. He also seemed uneasy, which Mr. Marsden put down to his having been caught lurking in the grounds of the house. The Marsdens returned to their house and the elder man telephoned the Police about their suspicious encounter.

When P.C. Ayres received the call, he went straightway to the Marsdens' and obtained details of the incident and a description of the prowler. He then went about the village looking for the strange man.

Shortly before midnight, Mr. and Mrs. Stallwood, who lived next door to Fred Brooks, returned from an outing. Mr. Stallwood parked his car in a yard at the back of his garden and walked up to his house. As he did so, he heard a loud moaning coming from his neighbours' house. His wife had also heard the same noise, and banging as well. The two of them rushed next door. Mrs. Stallwod looked through the letterbox of the door and was astounded to see Fred Brooks apparently groping his way down the stairs. Her husband, in the meantime, had gone to the rear of the house and had entered via the open back door. He followed the sound of the awful groaning and eventually found his neighbour lying at the foot of the stairs in the hallway.

Mr. Stallwood rolled the elderly man on to one side and he could see that old Mr. Brooks had terrible head wounds. Whilst his wife went to telephone for an ambulance and the Police, Mr. Stallwood tried to comfort Mr. Brooks. However, he died shortly before the emergency services arrived.

In the meantime, P.C. Ayres had been continuing his search around the village, and it was almost midnight, when, on an unlit footpath, he was alerted to the sound of footsteps approaching him. As whoever it was came up to him, P.C. Ayres switched on his torch and shone it in the direction of where the steps were coming from. He saw that it was someone he knew, George Castle. The Policeman could also see that the clothes he was wearing fitted the description given him by the Marsdens. As he let the beam of his torch play over the figure, he was surprised to see that Castle was carrying a bloodstained axe! Looking over him more closely, the Constable could see that there was blood on his mackintosh and on his face.

P.C. Ayres deftly took the axe from Castle's hand and enquired, "What have you done with this?"

"I hit old Fred Brooks with it," was the reply.

The village Constable suggested they go to his Police house. As they did so Castle removed his gloves and threw them down on the footpath. P.C. Ayres retrieved them. On their way Castle kept saying to his Police escort, "I thumped him. Don't ask me why."

When they arrived at the village Police house, Castle remarked, "This has been building up for five or six years. Don't ask me about it."

P.C.Ayres telephoned High Wycombe Police Station and asked for assistance, and a short time later Detective Sergeant Peter Apted arrived.

Seeing the blood on his face and on his clothing, the detective quite reasonably enquired, "What have you been up to?"

Castle replied, "Don't ask me. I've done old Fred Brooks. My wife will be worried, will you tell her where I am?"

After saying that she would be informed, Sergeant Apted asked, "What have you done to Brooks?"

Castle answered, "I don't know. I seem to remember speaking to someone in a car. The next thing I knew is I was lying with him at the bottom of the stairs. I heard someone shouting from outside as I got up and ran away."

Sergeant Apted produced the axe that his uniform colleague had seized, "Did you hit him with it?" he asked

"Yes," was the reply. "I must have done. It's my chopper."

The house where Fred Brooks was killed.

When the detective questioned him about the bloodstained clothing he had been wearing that warm summer night, Castle would only reply, "I don't know."

Sergeant Apted then left the Police house and went to 1, Council Cottages, where he saw the body of Fred Brooks and the dreadful wounds that had been inflicted on him, before returning to the Police house where he again confronted George Castle.

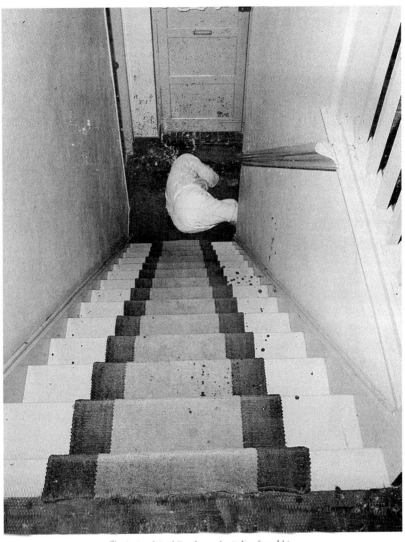

The body of Fred Brooks as the Police found him.

The Sergeant told the prisoner that he had visited 1, Council Cottages where he had seen the dead body of Fred Brooks, and the severe injuries that had been inflicted to his head. The detective added, "I have been told that you caused these injuries."

Castle replied, "I don't know what to say." He paused, then added, "He's dead, is he?"

Sergeant Apted answered, "Yes."

Castle continued, "All I remember is lying at the bottom of the stairs with him."

Castle was then taken to High Wycombe Police Station where he made a statement to Sergeant Apted and P.C. Ayres, part of which reads, "....I remember putting the kids to bed. I've got a faint recollection of talking to someone in a car. I went to Fred's house, I didn't go there to rob him, at least I don't think I did. I don't remember what happened at the house, I don't know why because I couldn't have been drunk. I don't remember whether there was a fight between Fred and me. All I remember is lying at the bottom of the stairs with him in a heap. I remember someone shouting from outside his house and I got up and ran away. The next thing I remember is a big light in my face and P.C. Ayres grabbed hold of me. I remember that I had a chopper in my hand........."

Later the same day, Detective Sergeant Apted charged Castle with the murder of Fred Brooks.

A search of Fred Brooks' house by Police revealed a large amount of money in his trousers' pockets, thus appearing to bear out what Castle had told the detectives, that robbery was not the motive, unless he had been disturbed by the Smallwoods before he could take the old man's money. Or, could something have occurred during his stay at Brooks' house that had caused Castle's mind to snap?

At his trial at Leicestershire Assizes later the same year, Castle was found not guilty of murder, by reason of insanity. Defence counsel produced evidence of Castle being in a state of automatism; that he did not know what he was doing, and this, the Prosecution was prepared to accept.

Doctors called by both the Defence and Prosecution had come to the conclusion that, at the time of the commission of the crime, Castle was not in his normal state of mind.

He was therefore ordered to be detained at Broadmoor Hospital.

"GO ON THEN, GET IT OVER WITH!"

Marlow - 1967

Fate is defined by the Concise Oxford Dictionary as, "a power regarded as predetermining events unalterably." Many people believe that certain things occur because they are ordained to happen, others disregard this notion.

Perhaps Fate decreed that a minor incident that happened some ten years or so beforehand would eventually lead to something, inevitably, tragically occurring several years later.

William 'Willy' Williams and Frederick Pritchard were driving a lorry in central London one day in the late 1950s, when they observed a teenaged girl standing by the kerbside crying. They stopped their vehicle and asked what the trouble was. The girl told them that she had run away from home. The two men, taking pity on her, offered her a lift in their lorry. They took her to Slough, where they left her in a flat at Stoke Poges opposite a cherry orchard. Also living there at the time and working in the orchard was a man known to both the men. He was Dennis Perry who came from Marlow, as did Willy Williams and Fred Pritchard.

Dennis Perry was not the most intelligent of men. He had suffered various illnesses when younger and as a consequence received little formal education and could neither read nor write. He was unkempt and scruffy. He had been married several years before, but the marriage had not worked out and he and his wife had separated. He was not the most prepossessing of men, but he was genuinely fond of children however.

It was only a short time later that Dennis and Pat, for that was the name of the girl found on the streets of London and deposited at Stoke Poges, decided that they would live together. This must have come as a surprise to most people as Perry was twenty years older than Pat.

Notwithstanding their age difference they lived together at Marlow, at first one address then another before, in early 1967, they settled in a house in Newfield Gardens. Pat had by now borne two children, a girl and a boy. On the outside, all seemed harmonious but there were tensions developing. Dennis could be violent, although not many people could say that he ever struck Pat or their children. One who could, however, was a teenager named David White.[1] He was a regular visitor to the Perrys and both Pat and Dennis were quite fond of him. He would say later that he had seen arguments between the two and also once when Dennis had thrown his young son across the room. David enjoyed Dennis' company, for he would take him rabbit shooting with the .410 shotgun that he owned.

Dennis, it would appear, slipped back into his slovenly ways and Pat, as she confided in a friend, was turned off by them. The way he ate for one thing, and if he did not like the meals she cooked for him, he would throw them away.

As David passed into adolescence he realised that he was falling in love with Pat and eventually she with him. When David proposed marriage, Pat accepted, having decided that life with Dennis was no longer appealing.

In the early autumn of 1967, Perry went round to Willy Williams' house. He showed him a note, which had been left by Pat ,and asked if Williams would read it to him. This his friend did and in it Pat stated that she had gone to Orpington, to her mother's, as she was ill.

Perry said that he wanted to go there to see if he could help, and Williams drove him there in his van. When they reached Orpington, Williams stayed outside, whilst Perry went inside the house. Williams could see that Pat and Dennis were having some sort of row, and when he left, carrying his son, Pat struck Dennis across the face. Perry walked off down the street. Pat walked over to the van and spoke to Williams. She was very upset at having her son snatched away. Williams went after Perry and attempted to persuade him to return the infant, but Perry refused and in the end Williams took both father and son back to Marlow.

1 Not his real name.

Pat went to Court to obtain an order awarding custody of the children to her and this was affirmed and Perry had also to pay maintenance to Pat as well. Perry was to take the boy to his mother on Sunday, 17th December and hand him over to her.

Just two days beforehand, David and Pat were married at Lewisham Registry Office. Fate was to decree that it would be a very short marriage indeed.

On the appointed day of the handover Dennis Perry told Williams that Pat had telephoned to say that she would be coming to Marlow to take the boy away with her.

That afternoon, Sergeant Connelly was on duty at Marlow Police Station when Pat White, as she now was, asked to see him. She produced a letter from her solicitors, which stated that the Court had given her legal custody of the children. Pat told the Sergeant that she intended going to Newfield Gardens to collect her son and some clothing from the house. She requested a Police presence whilst she did this.

These situations, 'domestics', as they are known to the Police, can be fraught with trouble, with the two protagonists arguing and shouting, for these matters are very seldom settled amicably, and the Police, in a well nigh impossible role, try to preserve some semblance of order.

Sergeant Connelly therefore said that he would accompany Pat, but added that he could not enter the house. The Police, he explained to her, would be there to prevent a breach of the peace. He emphasised that, if there was an argument inside the house, Pat was to leave immediately, and she would then have to refer the matter back to her solicitors. (This was an entirely civil matter and outside the jurisdiction of the Police.)

Having made quite sure that Pat understood this, the Sergeant obtained the services of a Woman Police Constable and took Pat in a Police car to Newfield Gardens. The Police Officer drove a few yards past the house where Pat and Dennis Perry had lived such a short time before, and as he did so he glanced up and could see a man in a lighted downstairs room. Sergeant Connelly parked the car a few yards away, reasoning that the sight of uniformed Police Officers might possibly inflame the situation further.

Pat got out of the car and the Police Sergeant warned her again that if there was any argument, or Perry would not give her the clothes, she was to leave and come straight out.

Pat nodded and walked off in the direction of the house. Sergeant Connelly watched as she opened the front gate and walked up the drive to the front door. A minute or so later he heard the sound of a door being slammed shut. Shortly after that he heard what sounded to him like a dustbin lid being placed heavily on a dustbin. The two Police Officers waited patiently in their car for Pat to return.

Willy Williams was, to say the least, surprised when Dennis Perry suddenly barged into his house via the back door. Propelling his little boy in as well, he breathlessly asked Mr. Williams to look after him.

"What's up then?" asked the somewhat bemused Williams.

"I've just shot Pat!" was the astounding response. With that Perry left the house.

With a friend Williams rushed over to Perry's house, passing the Police car as he did so.

"Come on," he called to the Police Officers, "he's shot her!"

Sergeant Connelly and the W.P.C. clambered out of their car and ran over to the house as well.

The front door was shut and the Sergeant carried on to the back door which was open.

Sergeant Connelly entered the house, going through the kitchen and into the hall. He could see the body of a woman lying on her back with a large pool of blood beneath her on the floor. There were splashes of blood on the wall and woodwork. Sergeant Connelly looked down at the woman he had so recently encountered and driven to the house and could plainly see a bloodied hole in her forehead. She lay perfectly still and it was obvious that she was dead.

The Policeman looked around and noticed a suitcase full of clothing, while across her legs was a large box containing a doll. Alongside the body was a child's tricycle. Sergeant Connelly contacted the Police Station, initiating the first steps into a murder investigation.

90

The body of Pat White.

uncle's wife. He then returned and saw that Dennis Perry was now in the garden and anxious to leave. David Savin talked to him calmly and persuaded him to return into the house and sit down, where Mrs. Savin made him a sandwich.

As he was eating it, one of Perry's uncles came into the house and wanted to know what his nephew had been up to. Dennis Perry, munching his sandwich, placed the shotgun between his legs and his uncle took the opportunity offered and seized the deadly weapon as another of Perry's uncles entered the room and wrestled with him. In a manoeuvre agreed beforehand and to minimalise the risk of possible injury caused by the firing of the shotgun, the Police, headed by Detective Sergeant Peter Apted, now entered and secured their prisoner.

The Savin family left their house, no doubt thankful that the danger they had been placed in and which they had so admirably coped with was now over.

When Perry realised that further struggle was useless, he capitulated and was taken to Marlow Police Station.

Sat in the rear of the Police car next to Sergeant Apted, he confided to his captor, "This wouldn't have happened if she had let me see my daughter. I told her I'd blow her head off and she just said, 'Go on then.'" Perry then said, "Why did you have to stop me? I was going to put the gun in my mouth and blow my head off after I got 'Whitey.'"

At the Police Station Dennis Perry was interviewed by Police Officers and made a statement, detailing part of the conversation between him and Pat "...'Well if you can't bring her (referring to their daughter) to see me, you aren't taking the boy.' She said, 'It will be over my dead body if I can't take him.' I said, 'Well it will be then.' I said, 'Well I'll blow your head off.' She said, 'Go on then.' I went and got the gun from the front room. I got a cartridge for it from my jacket pocket....and loaded the gun. I went out into the hall. She was still stood there where she was before. I said, 'Here it is then.' She said, ' Go on then, get it over with.' I said, 'Right.' I pointed the gun at her head. She was about a yard away. I just shot her....."

Perry was charged with Pat's murder. He appeared at Leicester Assizes the following year and pleaded not guilty to murder, and the prosecution evidence was heard. Perry then went into the witness box and said that, when his partner had telephoned on that fateful day, she had said that she would collect their son, bringing their daughter with her. Perry had thought she was coming back to him for good, but when she arrived at the house, he could see that she had not brought their daughter with her. Pat had then said that they were all going abroad. Perry stated that he had told her that, if she would not let him see their daughter, she could not have the boy. Pat had then said, 'Over my dead body', to which he had responded, 'That could be arranged.' Perry then said that Pat had answered, 'Get on with it then.' He had loaded the gun, but only to frighten her, but she had said, 'Come on! Get it over with. I don't want to stand here all day.' He remembered pointing the gun at her, and then it was all over and he had taken the boy and left the house.

Perry collapsed in the witness box, and the case was adjourned until he had recovered. When he returned to the Court, he changed his plea to guilty to manslaughter, and this was accepted by the Prosecution. Mr. Justice Veale, in sentencing Perry to eight years imprisonment, commented that it was a bad case of manslaughter.

A PUPPY'S TALE

Stokenchurch - 1972

When Alan Main caught a wandering dog in High Wycombe town centre on 4th February, 1972, he decided, with all the best intentions in the world no doubt, to take it to the local Police Station so that it would be out of harm's way, as it had almost caused an accident. Had Mr. Main known that his public-spirited action would lead to murder, he might have ignored the dog and let it run away.

The Police Constable behind the counter took the dog from Mr. Main, made an entry in the stray dog register and shortly after handed it over to Clement Blois, of Hall Bottom Kennels, Stokenchurch, who drove off with the dog in his estate car. Blois, known as Bob, had served in the Police but had resigned and now ran the kennels at Stokenchurch on the outskirts of High Wycombe, where, in addition to his other work, he looked after the stray dogs handed in at the Police Station. He would hold them for seven days, unless they were claimed beforehand, then hand them over to a Pet Rescue Service.

Later the same day, another man called at the Police Station, saying that he had lost his dog and gave the Constable a description of the wandering animal which corresponded to the one that had been recently handed in. The Constable said that it was too late to collect the dog on that day, but that, if he called back the following day with the sum of £1.20p, he would be given a receipt and would then be told where the dog was kennelled.

The next afternoon the man returned to the Police Station and enquired as to the amount he owed for the return of the dog. The Constable told him again, £1.20p.

"I haven't got the money now," the man informed the Constable, "but I will get some and come in tomorrow." "In that case," the Constable replied, "bring in £1.80 as that will cost you another day's keep." The man then asked at which kennels the dog was being kept, but the Constable was not falling for that trick. "You will be given a receipt when you bring the money in and then told where to go and collect your dog."

A few minutes after this conversation had taken place at the Police Station, Mrs. Pitcher, who owned some kennels in High Wycombe heard a loud knock on the door. When she went to answer the door, she spoke to two men who were enquiring about a Terrier dog, which they believed had been brought in the previous day. Mrs. Pitcher informed them that no such dog had been brought to her kennels.

Suddenly Mrs. Pitcher heard the noise of a gate being closed and, as she glanced up, she saw two girls approaching. As they hurried across the yard both appeared to be very angry.

One of the men asked, "This is Hall Bottom Kennels, isn't it?"

"No," Mrs. Pitcher replied. "Hall Bottom Kennels are at Stokenchurch."

The men and the girls walked over to their car parked outside the garage. As they did so, one of the girls employed by Mrs. Pitcher attempted to settle the barking dogs held at the kennels by banging on their door. "Stop banging on the door, you'll make them more frightened than ever," one of the female visitors called out. When the kennel girl said, "Pardo," the young woman shouted again, "Stop banging that door." Mrs. Pitcher and her kennel girl were nonplussed and the young woman said, "I hate some people. I can't stand some people." The four visitors got into their car and drove off.

After that little contretemps, Mrs. Pitcher deemed it wise to telephone Mrs. Blois and forewarn her of the visit she could expect.

When Mrs. Blois received the call, she glanced out of the window and noticed two men and two women approaching. She saw them go round to the rear of the house, and her husband Bob put on his wellington boots and went out to see his visitors. The two girls had gone through a gate into the exercise compounds, having ignored a 'No Entry' sign. Bob shouted after them, "Hey, come out of there." The two girls came back.

Bob wanted to know what they were doing, and one of them replied that they wanted their dog. Bob pointed out that if it was a stray dog they should have called at the Police Station. The same girl retorted that it was not a stray; that someone had let it out of the

Hall Bottom Kennels, Stokenchurch.

caravan in which they lived. One of the girls attempted to push past Bob, but he stopped her. She then started using foul language towards him and Mrs. Blois went back to the house to telephone the Police, as she anticipated trouble.

The Blois' twelve-year-old son, Martin, and his friend stayed and watched the row. Once again the girl tried to walk past Bob, but he caught hold of her arm and swung her around, pushing her over. She got up swearing at him. Bob Blois was by now talking to one of the men. The girl advanced upon the kennel owner with a knife in her hand. She struck out once at Bob but missed, then she struck again. This time the knife went into Bob's chest. The girl calmly withdrew the knife and put it in her pocket and stood back. Bob Blois again told her that she would have to get a receipt before she could have the dog. He then collapsed!

One of the men was heard to say, "Now look what you have done, come on, run." The four intrusive visitors ran off. Young Martin Blois went to his father who lay quite still on the ground. The boy could see blood on his father's shirt and he ran in to tell his mother what had happened. When Mrs. Blois saw her husband, she straightaway telephoned the Ambulance and the Police, but it was too late. Bob Blois was dead!

That afternoon, W.P.C. Sheila Cornish spoke to Lynne Stroud and Peter Smith who had called at Marlow Police Station. At the time Stroud was using the surname Smith, stating that she was married to the man she accompanied. The Police Officer asked what they wanted to see her about. Smith replied, "She wants to tell you that she lost her temper and stabbed someone." Stroud butted in, "I didn't mean it, I just lost my temper." She then related to W.P.C. Cornish her version of the events that had occurred at Hall Bottom Kennels earlier that day. She said that she had been pushed over in the mud and that she had pulled her knife from her boot, shouting, "I'll bloody kill you, you bastard!" Her foot had then slipped in the mud and she had lurched forward, and the knife had gone into the top of Bob Blois' jacket. She hadn't thought it had gone into his body. They had all run

Hall Bottom Kennels, where Bob Blois confronted his killer.

off when they had heard a woman scream, "You've killed him!" As they had run away, Stroud had looked at the knife, saw that it had blood on it and had thrown it away. Stroud was now interviewed by Detective Superintendent Joe Coffey and Detective Inspector (later Chief Superintendent) Ray Tilly, but she stuck to the story she had told the W.P.C. A search was made of the undergrowth near the kennels and the knife was recovered where Stroud had said she had discarded it.

Detective Inspector Tilly was not satisfied that Stroud was telling the complete truth and reinterviewed her partner, Smith. Under further questioning he admitted that Stroud had made two downward stabbing blows towards Bob Blois and also that she had neither fallen forward nor had she slipped in the mud. They had been deliberate blows. He told the Inspector more; that on the way to Marlow Police Station he and Stroud had concocted the story that she had fallen on Bob Blois. He also said that he and Stroud were not married, they just lived together.

Detective Inspector Tilly now decided that it was time to speak to Stroud again. Mentioning that he now knew that they were not married as she had insisted, she replied, "....I suppose he told you everything else as well." "About what?" the Inspector enquired. "That we'd say I slipped." "Wasn't it an accident like you said then?" Inspector Tilly asked. Stroud replied, "Look, I wanted my bloody dog back. He wouldn't give me it and threw me on the ground. I lost my temper and stabbed him. Any normal person would have got out of the way, wouldn't you? I'd still do it again...I'll plead insanity and then I'll have to go to Holloway for a medical. I still say I'd do it again." Chillingly she added, "If they give my dog away, I'll get them, even if I have to wait ten years." The Detective Inspector realised that there was no further point in discussing the matter and later Stroud was charged with the murder of Bob Blois.

At the Old Bailey later the same year Stroud pleaded not guilty to that indictment but guilty to manslaughter on the grounds of diminished responsibility. After listening to the outline of the case,

101

'Rusty', over whom Bob Blois was killed.

and hearing from the Senior Medical Officer from Holloway Prison that Stroud was suffering from a psychopathic disorder, Sir Carl Aarvold, the Recorder of London, ordered that she be sent to Broadmoor for an unlimited time.

Det. Insp. Ray Tilly, who interviewed the killer of Bob Blms.

A FRIEND INDEED!

Aylesbury - 1977

The late 1970s saw the era of the punk rockers who, with their outrageous clothing, music, facial adornments, language and behaviour encouraged young people to rebel against all things and all people in authority. Of course, teenagers for many years had been rebelling against authority. This was simply the latest manifestation of a world that seemed, to most people over the age of forty, to be rushing into anarchy.

In October 1977 when a punk rock group were playing a 'gig' at Aston Clinton therefore, it seemed perfectly natural for some teenagers who stood in awe of their idols to want to go and worship at their feet. One such was a fourteen-year girl, Jackie Ludlow, who lived with her mother and step-father at Long Crendon. She pleaded with her step-father to be allowed to see the group playing, but he put his foot down and said, quite frankly, that he would not let her go. A row ensued and eventually Jackie, with all the forcefulness that a fourteen year old can muster, stated that she was going around to her grandmother's house. When an impasse has been reached, a cooling off period can often be a good thing. A close friend of the family, Stephen Willis, offered to take Jackie there, and in her haste to get away from the family house Jackie accepted. To Mrs. Baldwin, Jackie's mother, Willis, a 22-year-old labourer, was a kind and gentle man whom she had known for years. He bought toys for the children, and in her own words Mrs. Baldwin described him as "...a bit like an uncle." Jackie and Willis left the house at 9.40pm that day. It was the last time that Mrs. Baldwin was to see Jackie alive!

When she did not show up at her grandmother's house nor return home, the Baldwins became alarmed and notified the Police. All reports of reports of missing children and young persons are treated seriously by the Police, and detailed searching and enquiries of witnesses are carried out as a matter of course, especially when the missing youngster does not return within a few hours. Stephen Willis was therefore detained on suspicion of abduction and interviewed, as he had been the last person to see Jackie that night. He maintained that she had suddenly jumped out of his car, saying that that she was going to run away. A thorough search of his house was made by the Police and eventually, when they were quite satisfied that Jackie was not on the premises, one way or another, they left. However, after the Police had conducted their search of Willis' house, a neighbour saw him do something rather out of the ordinary. He was seen to cut down the fencing around his house in order that he could drive his car right up to the front door.

Jackie's description was widely circulated both locally and nationally, and her details were given to the press, along with that of the clothing and jewellery that she had been wearing on the night of October 7th. It was all to no avail, and Jackie remained on the missing person file.

In January of the following year, a man searching for scrap metal along the Old Stocklake Road on the outskirts of Aylesbury thought he saw something of interest in a water logged ditch running parallel to the road. He peered more closely and saw, to his horror, that it was the naked body of a young female. He hurried to report the finding to the Police, who responded immediately to the call.

When it was ascertained that the girl had died an unnatural death, the Criminal Investigation Department were informed, and a full scale murder investigation was commenced by Detective Superintendent Lawson with Detective Chief Inspector Maurice Caro. A post mortem examination conducted by Professor Keith Mant was performed, and the cause of death was given as strangulation. It was also definitely established that it was the body of Jackie Ludlow.

Stephen Willis was now questioned by the two senior detectives about what had happened the night that Jackie had disappeared. He told them that, as he was taking Jackie to her grandmother's, she had run off, only to show up two hours later at his house, where she stayed the night. He was taking her home the next day, he continued, when she had started screaming, and he had put his hands around her neck to stop her. "...I had no intention of killing her," he informed the detectives. "I just wanted to stop the noise. My head was bursting and I stopped the car. She kept on screaming, so I shook her to stop the noise, but she kept on screaming, and I put my hands round her neck and strangled her."

Willis added that he had sat in his car for half an hour before he realised that the girl was dead. He told the Police that he had then driven home and had put her body under the settee in the front room. He added that the body had still been there when the Police had searched the place, but they had not found her. This claim was most emphatically rejected by the Police Officers who had conducted the search. They maintained that they had searched the house thoroughly, and Jackie's body was not at the house.

After the Police had left, Willis went on, he had cut down the fence around his house with a hacksaw so that he could drive his car up to the front door and load her body into it. He had stripped the clothes and jewellery from her body, before throwing it into the ditch where it had been found some months later. He had returned home and had placed Jackie's clothing and jewellery on a bonfire. The Police raked over the ashes of the fire and discovered the remains of some love beads that Jackie had been wearing on her necklace.

Later that year, Willis appeared at Reading Crown court, where he was found guilty of the murder of Jackie Ludlow. "You have been found guilty of a murder of a singularly unpleasant kind," intoned Mr. Justice Stocker, before sentencing Willis to life imprisonment.

THE INCREDIBLE HULK

Newport Pagnell - 1982

(The offender in this case used many aliases. I have used his real name throughout to avoid confusion.)

PART ONE

For Albert Protheroe of Llandovery, Dyfed, a pensioner, the year 1982 got off to a bad start. Until 1980 he had shared his home in the High Street with his housekeeper Gladys Roberts. She had left when she had married a farmer, becoming Mrs. Price[1], and had gone to live with her husband at Pontardawe. However, just before Christmas 1981, Mrs. Price had quarrelled with her husband and had gone back to Llandovery, asking Mr. Protheroe if she could stay with him. He had readily agreed.

On the last day of the old year, Albert checked the savings he held in an old tobacco tin hidden in a chest of drawers in his bedroom. He counted the £10 and £20 notes and noted, with some satisfaction, that he now had £600. He carefully replaced the tin in its hiding place. The next day, January 1st 1982, he left Llandovery to visit a friend for a few days.

That night, feeling lonely and in need of some company, Mrs. Price decided to visit The Red Lion in Llandovery, and whilst there she met a 35 year old man, David Hampshire, and engaged him in conversation. He told her that he was sleeping rough, and Mrs. Price, feeling rather sorry for him, offered him the use of Mr. Protheroe's bed for a few nights, a proposal he accepted with alacrity. Hampshire remained at 50 High Street, Llandovery for three nights, leaving early on Monday, 4th January.

That same day, Albert Protheroe returned from his short holiday and one of the first things he did was to look in his chest of drawers for the tobacco tin containing his money. He was more than a little surprised to find that his cache was missing. When he mentioned this to Mrs. Price she admitted that she had allowed a stranger to stay at the house for a few days and make use of the temporarily empty bed.

1 Not her real name.

107

He must have looked around the room, found the money and taken it with him when he departed. If Albert Protheroe, with some justification, felt aggrieved at his loss, at least it was only money. Others who encountered David Hampshire were to lose much, much more.

Hampshire decided that Llandovery was not a good place to stay and left hurriedly for pastures new. On the evening of January 5th he walked into a hotel in Shrewsbury, where he stayed for three nights and then left for Cherry Hinton, Cambridgeshire, remaining there for the next two nights. He then managed to obtain a lift to Newport Pagnell and stayed at a house owned by Mrs. Graydon, the landlady of the Rose and Crown public house. To the people who met him he presented a somewhat pathetic appearance, trying to sell various items, going to the Social Security offices, in fact a loner who would engage anyone in conversation who showed him any sympathy.

It was whilst he was at the Rose and Crown during the evening of Wednesday, 13th January, that he was seen playing pool with Julie Ann Deakin, an 18 year old girl who lived with a friend, Hazel Busby, at 54, Glenwoods, a small middle of terraced house which was owned by a third party and rented out to them.

Whatever conversation took place between these two totally different persons one thing is certain. Hampshire managed to persuade Julie to allow him to stay at her house. She phoned Hazel, asking if she would mind if a man slept on their couch. Hazel agreed, and Julie and Hampshire left the Rose and Crown after he had bought a bottle of cider and a quarter bottle of whisky. When the pair arrived at 54, Glenwoods, they sat down with Hazel and talked all night.

The next day, whilst Julie was at work, Hampshire and Hazel talked and played cards through the afternoon. He asked if he could remain at their house for a further week, but Hazel would not agree, although she said he could stay for one more night. That evening, Hampshire, Julie and Hazel walked to the Rose and Crown, had a few drinks and returned home.

On Friday, 15th January both girls left for work, meeting later when Julie told her friend that Hampshire would be going after she had given him a dinner, which she prepared as soon as she arrived at the house and took upstairs to her bedroom for him.

Shortly after, Julie's parents arrived and, whilst they waited for their daughter, Hazel gave them a glass of sherry from a bottle which she had bought that evening. Mr. and Mrs. Deakin then took Julie to a public house in Stony Stratford where they had dinner.

After Julie had left with her parents, Hazel, with the assistance of a friend, had persuaded Hampshire to leave 54, Glenwoods, and he walked round to the Rose and Crown public house. Hazel and her friend also left the house, locking the back door and leaving the key on the work surface nearby. A short time later Julie returned to the house after being dropped off by her parents.

Hampshire, meanwhile, was making himself obnoxious to customers in the Rose and Crown by boasting of his sexual adventures with different females. He left the pub after buying a small bottle of light ale, and he was observed a few minutes later by passers-by in Glenwoods.

At approximately 12.30am Hazel phoned the house, but, when she received no reply, she assumed that Julie was still out with her parents. Hazel eventually returned about half-an-hour later and noticed a figure moving about. At first she thought it was Julie, although afterwards she admitted that she could not be sure. She sat down and listened to some music for over an hour before going to bed. She was a little mystified by seeing that the back door key she had placed on the work surface earlier was now missing, as was the bottle of sherry she had bought that evening.

Mrs. Graydon of the Rose and Crown had a rather rude awakening early on Saturday morning when a barking dog roused her from her slumber. When she got up to see why the dog had been disturbed, she found David Hampshire at the side door of the public house asking for the return of the possessions he had left in the room she had let to him a few days before. As Mrs. Graydon handed them over to Hampshire, he mentioned to her that he intended to hitch a lift from the nearby M1 Motorway Service Area.

In this he was evidently successful, for on that afternoon he was

Glenwoods, Newport Pagnall, where Julie Ann Deakin met her death

seen at Holyhead Market attempting to sell some clogs and a leather jacket, in an effort to raise the price of a ticket for the ferry to Ireland. Later the same evening he was seen in the Dublin Packet public house selling clothing for the same reason. That he managed to do so was evidenced by his being on the 3.15am boat, sailing from Holyhead to Dun Loaghire.

Back at Newport Pagnell meanwhile, Hazel had risen about 11.30 am and, after doing some housework, had gone out on two occasions, not unduly worried by the non-appearance of her housemate. By 6.30pm she had become concerned enough to call up the stairs. When she received no reply she walked up and knocked on Julie's bedroom door. There was still no answer. Hazel did not however, open the door, nor did she enter the room.

Hazel now went out for the evening, encountering two male friends to whom she confided that she felt something was wrong. At 10pm that night the threesome went to 54, Glenwoods and one of Hazel's friends called out to Julie. Again there was no response and, on entering the bedroom, he could see Julie's head just above the bedclothes. Believing that she was asleep, he returned downstairs. This still did not quieten the suspicions that the three friends had, and the other man, thinking this was most peculiar, decided that he had better look for himself. Going into Julie's room he walked right over to the bed and took a closer look. He observed dried blood on her pale face and, on holding up her hand, noticed that it felt very cold and there was no pulse. He realised that Julie was dead and telephoned the Police.

An initial inspection revealed that Julie had been strangled by a pair of her own tights, and a murder enquiry was put under way, led by Detective Superintendent Roger Sillence, assisted by Detective Inspector Norman Robson with officers of the Serious Crime Squad and local Police.

A minute examination of the house was carried out, and numerous items were removed from there and the scene immediately outside for further forensic scrutiny. Amongst these articles was a bottle of sherry and a bottle of light ale which had, no doubt, been handled by the offender.

Det. Superintendent Roger Sillence, Senior Investigator into two horrific murders.

From the various witnesses a good description of the man Julie had met at the Rose and Crown was obtained. He was described as 6 feet six inches tall, medium build, brown hair and wearing gold framed spectacles. The only thing missing was his name. The examination of the various items found at or near the house would no doubt yield fingerprints, which would eventually give the identity of the suspect, but this would take time, even if he had a criminal record.

However, one of the local C.I.D. officers, Frank Sullivan, recalled an incident he and a colleague had attended in Newport Pagnell two years before, when they had dealt with an allegation of indecency. The two Policemen had interviewed one David Hampshire and, although nothing had come of the incident and Hampshire had been released, Detective Constable Sullivan, later Superintendent, remembered his name and description and the fact that he had a substantial criminal record, including convictions for indecent assault on females. He passed the name onto Superintendent Sillence, and photographs of this suspect were shown to various witnesses who readily identified him. The hunt was now on for David Hampshire in the earnest hope that he would be traced before he struck again. Hampshire's photograph was given to the press who, because of his sheer physical presence, was dubbed 'The Hulk', after a character in a popular television series that was appearing about the time.

Witnesses now came forward who recalled Hampshire being in Holyhead and catching the ferry to Dun Laoghire. But where had he gone to? Was he in Dublin haunting the many bars in that city or had he gone farther afield into one of the other cities of the Irish Republic? Or had he gone into hiding in deep country?

PART TWO

In the wild and lonely country of County Cork there are many bays and inlets along the coast where visitors, entranced by the sheer beauty, have decided to purchase a second home in which to spend their holidays. One such holiday home had been purchased by a German at Agherdown at Roaring Water Bay. Although occupied

113

MURDER

The man pictured below is sought in connection with the murder of an 18 year old girl at Newport Pagnell, on January 15/16, 1982.

HAVE YOU SEEN THIS MAN?

35 years, 6 ft. 8 in., medium build, light brown hair, gold framed spectacles, last seen wearing tan ankle boots, combat jumper and jeans, carrying a haversack

IF SO, PLEASE CONTACT YOUR LOCAL POLICE STATION OR THE MURDER INCIDENT ROOM AT NEWPORT PAGNELL

RING (0908) 610222

'Wanted' posters, issued by the press, assisted a Nationwide Hunt for the killer of Julie Ann Deakin.

during the summer months, in the winter it was left alone. The local people of course would know when anyone was in residence and when it should be empty and so, when a strange man was seen coming from the house in the depth of winter, it was, naturally, noticed. When the man approached a 10 year old boy and asked him where the local shop was, the lad, recognising him from the picture and description circulated in the Irish press as 'The Hulk' and wanted by the English Police for questioning in connection with a murder, pointed him in the wrong direction, then ran to the shop himself and telephoned the local Guarda Station at Skibereen. Guarda Sergeant John Breen and Detective Guarda John McCarthy decided to investigate.

The man was pointed out to them, and, after a short chase, was captured by the two Irish Policemen. He admitted to them that his name was David Hampshire and the fact that he had broken into the house, removing the putty from around the window and replacing it, when he had entered, in an effort to put people off his track. However, when he emerged to purchase some milk, he had been spotted and the matter reported. When he was asked how he had managed to arrive in this isolated place, Hampshire replied that he had thumbed a lift from Dublin with a nurse, who obviously was in complete ignorance of the fact that she was assisting a man wanted in connection with a murder.

Hampshire went on that he had met Julie Deakin in Newport Pagnell but would not admit to killing her. He was charged with breaking into the house and theft, and was remanded in custody.

Detective Inspector Robson and Detective Constable Brian Bedwell were promptly despatched to the Irish Republic to interview Hampshire, and in the Guarda Station at Clonakilty he finally admitted to the two detectives that he had murdered Julie a few weeks previously.

There was now the formality of Hampshire appearing before the local court for the housebreaking charge. When he did so, he was given a suspended prison sentence for the offence.

He was not allowed to go free of course but was re-arrested and placed back before the Court, where the presiding Judge heard evidence of the English murder and, after examining the relevant papers, ordered his extradition to Britain.

It was whilst being conveyed back to the United Kingdom that Hampshire casually informed the accompanying detectives of another serious matter. On his arrival at Newport Pagnell Police Station he was interrogated at some length by Superintendent Sillence and Inspector Robson. He freely confessed to the murder of Julie Deakin. In Mr Sillence's own words, "He admitted the murder in a cold, almost disinterested manner." Hampshire now wanted to clear up another outstanding matter.

PART THREE

Zofia Noworol was a nineteen year old Polish citizen who had relatives in this country; an uncle, Father Slepokura, a Polish born Catholic priest living in Peterborough, and a cousin, Urszula Bednaczyk of Finchley, North London. In 1978 Zofia journeyed to England and worked as an 'au pair' in Finchley. In 1980 she travelled to Bournemouth, where she enrolled at the Southbourne School of English, but later worked as a washer-up at one of the many hotels in the area. It was in Bournemouth she encountered David Hampshire who was working as a builder's labourer.

In the late summer of 1980 Zofia's work permit expired, which meant that she would have to return to her home country. She travelled up to London, accompanied by Hampshire, and met Father Slepokura. The three of them went to Urszula Bednaczyk's home, where Zofia and her uncle stayed the night whilst Hampshire went elsewhere. The following morning Hampshire called at Urszula's house and, with her and Zofia, went to Victoria Railway Station where Zofia caught the boat train for the continent. Later that year Hampshire travelled to Poland himself, staying over the Christmas and New Year period before returning to this country.

In 1981, Hampshire, having obtained a further travel visa from the Polish Embassy, left England on 20th June. The Polish authorities extended the time limit on his visa, but Hampshire was eventually repatriated by the British Embassy in Warsaw in August, having run out of money.

At the end of that month Father Slepokura answered a telephone call from Hampshire, when he informed him that Zofia had disappeared whilst he had been staying in Poland. Receiving a similar telephone call in November, Father Slepokura asked if he could meet Hampshire to discuss the mystery of Zofia's disappearance, but Hampshire refused.

Hampshire also telephoned Urszula Bednacyzk, informing her that Zofia had vanished. Cousin Urszula made her own enquiries with her relations, and it was confirmed to her that Zofia had indeed gone missing on the 15th August, whilst she had been holidaying with Hampshire.

Quite unknown to her by now apprehensive relatives, Hampshire, on his return to this country, had visited a woman friend of his, a Miss Butler[2], and had sold her a Russian camera, which it later transpired had belonged to Zofia. Whilst with Miss Butler he appeared agitated and told her that he had strangled a man whilst he had been in Poland and buried his body in a wood.

Leaving Miss Butler, Hampshire moved around the country, recounting to various people that the Polish authorities were after him or that he had killed a man in that country. To one woman he encountered he gave a girl's leather shoulder bag.

He now admitted to the detectives that he had murdered Zofia!

Eventually, he continued, his meanderings led him to Llandovery, where he stole £600 belonging to Mr. Protheroe and thence to Newport Pagnell where he met Julie Deakin.

The two detectives, who had listened dispassionately to this story of two vicious murders, told nonchalantly by the huge man sat across the table from them and written down in statement form, now placed Hampshire in the cells. Despite his confession, Superintendent Sillence and Inspector Robson realised that they still had a lot of work to do before Hampshire faced a Judge.

A search of Hampshire's property revealed that he was in possession of pubic hair, which he alleged he had taken from Zofia's

---

2 Not her real name.

117

body. There were also some photograph negatives which, when developed, showed Zofia with a shoulder bag identical to the one Hampshire had given away and which the Police had recovered from the woman he had presented it to. Items of Julie's underwear, which Hampshire informed the detectives he had placed in a rainwater down pipe at 54, Glenwoods, were recovered, as was Julie's cigarette lighter, which had been secreted in the roof timbers in a disused coal shed in Caldecotte Street, Newport Pagnell, on the night of the murder.

Enquiries were also commenced with the Polish authorities and Zofia's body was found in some woods near Miesdrovjeve. She had been strangled during sexual intercourse.

In November 1982, Hampshire appeared at Northampton Crown Court where he pleaded "Not guilty" to the two murders but "Guilty" to manslaughter on the grounds of diminished responsibility. These pleas were accepted by the prosecution.

After the prosecution had outlined the facts behind the killings and the brutal way the two young women had met their deaths, Mr. Michael Connell defending said that Hampshire suffered from a chromosomal disorder. He was an 'XYY' man, who was less able to deal with stresses and strains and was totally unable to cope if taunts were made about his size. This chromosomal disorder had, with an excess of alcohol, led to the killing of Julie Deakin, whilst he, Hampshire, had believed that Zofia had been carrying on with a Polish Army Captain and had taunted him. "My mind went all red. I wanted to destroy her," he had told the Police in his statement. Superintendent Sillence knew, from the enquiries that he had made of the two women Hampshire had married and who had divorced him, that he also subjected them to a horrifying sequence of sexual abuse.

The Judge, Mr. Justice Drake, having received the medical reports on Hampshire, said, "You have a condition of mind which means that you are not on occasions fully responsible for your own actions. These were terrible killings of the two women concerned. It is clear that on occasions you give way to a terrible sexual desire and then

118

commit terrible sexual acts on the women with whom you are having intercourse. You did these killings because of your mental condition. This is a case not only for punishment but also where I must protect the public...the medical reports conclude that you are not capable of responding to psychiatric treatment. I consider that you present a grave threat to the public..."

Mr. Justice Drake thereupon sentenced Hampshire to imprisonment for life.

MURDER OF A PEACE WOMAN

Denham - 1984

Denham, in south Buckinghamshire, for all its prettiness has had, over the years, a number of gruesome murders committed there. One has only to think of the Marshall family, virtually annihilated in 1870[1], the Plumridge murder of 1886[2], and the unsolved murder of Joyce Vera Green in 1958[3]. There have, unfortunately, been others. Quite why this picturesque village has been host to these murderous activities is unknown, perhaps it is its proximity to the sprawling mass of London and that in these quiet country lanes and by-ways it is easy to dispose of the bodies of victims. But of course, that only explains part of the mystery.

In 1984, Denham was to play host to yet another murder. In December of that year, the body of a woman was found near the 16th green of Denham Golf Course by a woman exercising her dog. Her first assumption was that it was a tailor's dummy. It is still very unusual even today to find bodies! However, when the lady returned and made a closer inspection, it was seen to be the corpse of a woman.

The Police duly attended and confirmed that indeed it was a dead female, and that she had been subjected to a very serious assault. Although she had not been raped, her body had been severely mutilated. She was wearing only her socks. Detective Superintendent Roger Nicklin of Thames Valley Police arrived and took charge of the investigation of the crime.

The pathologist, who performed a detailed post mortem examination, ascertained that the victim had been beaten around the head and then strangled. These were the injuries inflicted upon her, which had so appalled the Police Officers who had visited the site. When the scene of the crime was examined it appeared that she had been taken to the golf course and dragged to where she had later been discovered.

1 See 'Murder in Buckinghamshire' by the author.
2 See 'Buckinghamshire Murders' by the author.
3 See 'Murder in Buckinghamshire' by the author.

It was of paramount importance that the identity of the victim be ascertained, and it was soon established that she was Deidre Sainsbury, the daughter of a very prominent psychiatrist. She was active in the Greenham Common Peace Campaign that was taking place at the time[1]. She was single and had been visiting friends in London, leaving them on Saturday 22nd. December. She had not told them where she was going. She had then, it transpired later, hitched a lift from a passing motorist.

It was against this background that the Police commenced their enquiries. It was not a promising start, for the chances of clearing up a murder, probably committed by a passing motorist who has given a casual hitch-hiker a lift, are extremely remote. Nevertheless, the detectives set to work in an effort to ascertain who had committed this foul deed.

They interviewed people who had been attending Denham Golf Course during the evening when the body had been unceremoniously deposited. A number of persons were seen who had noticed a car in the lane where Deirdre's body was later found. Descriptions of the vehicle were taken from these witnesses. They varied, as no one had paid too much attention to a car in the middle of the night. One of them, however, was insistent that the car had a vinyl roof. This was duly noted, and the statements were handed in to the Incident Room for the perusal of the Senior Investigating Officer and his team.

Detective Superintendent Nicklin spoke to the media about the murder. This proved to be a shrewd move by the officer. Because of Denham's proximity to London, it was given full coverage in the media, national as well as local. It was as a result of this publicity that a man came forward with some very interesting information. He was duly interviewed by detectives, who quickly realised the importance of what he had to tell them. In fact, had someone attempted to pass it off in a work of fiction it would have been derided as too far fetched.

He had, he said, been standing on the North Circular Road on 22nd December. He was reading an article in a magazine about the

---

1 At this time a number of women were mounting a vigil outside the United States Air Force base at Greenham Common, near Newbury, protesting against the storing of nuclear weapons there.

dangers of women hitch-hiking. Glancing up at the passing traffic he noticed a young woman doing just that. He then observed a car pull up, the passenger door pushed open and the driver speak to the female hitch-hiker. He watched as she got into the car and the vehicle then drove off.

Shaking his head in disbelief at what he had seen, especially after having just read the article on this dangerous practice, the witness to this little incident wrote down the registration number of the car. He produced it to the detectives. He did not know if it was of any help to them of course but...

The interviewing detectives could hardly contain their excitement at this turn of events. Not only had this witness come forward; not only had he seen a very suspicious incident take place; not only could he describe the car and the woman who had so eagerly got into the passenger side of the vehicle; but he had TAKEN THE NUMBER OF THE CAR! It is at times like these that Police Officers feel like getting up, going over to the witness, kissing him or her on both cheeks, and awarding them the Croix de Guerre avec Palmes, so rarely does this sort of thing happen..

A check was made on the owner of the vehicle. It was ascertained that it had been driven by Colin Campbell, a 37-year-old sales representative. He was soon traced to an address in Newbury, and a team of detectives went to see him. His address was searched and a rucksack and leather passport holder, which was later proved to belong to Miss Sainsbury, was found. His car was seized and examined. It was seen to have a vinyl roof. The statement of the one witness, who had been leaving Denham Golf Course and who had noticed that the car he had seen had a vinyl roof, was then recalled. Campbell was arrested and charged with the murder of Deidre Sainsbury.

In July of 1985, Campbell appeared at Reading Crown Court and pleaded "Not guilty". His defence was that he had given Miss Sainsbury a lift in his car, then he had made advances to her when they had stopped in a quiet country lane. She had rejected him and he had panicked and had strangled her. He had then mutilated her body to make it look like the work of a madman.

After a three-day trial, he was found guilty. Mr. Justice Jones, in sentencing Campbell to the mandatory sentence of life imprisonment, said, "I have no doubt as to the verdict, which has not taken you by surprise in any way at all. The murder was unprovoked. It was a brutal, pointless murder."

Campbell had to be assisted from the dock. His wife burst into tears as he was taken away, and his mother shouted out, "You are cruel! See what you have done to him!" before she was led away. She was lucky; she had not seen the photographs of the body of Deidre Sainsbury.

In November, of 1986, Campbell lost his appeal against his conviction for murder.

MURDER IN THE CHILTERNS

ST. LEONARDS - 1989

High in the Chiltern Hills overlooking the Vale of Aylesbury lies the small village of St. Leonards. This almost isolated community surrounded by woods is only occasionally disturbed by the outside world - the odd car being driven through from Chesham to Wendover or beyond, or the silent, swooping gliders from nearby Halton seeking the thermals to keep them aloft

Graham and Julia Barrett lived with their two children in what Police would describe in their reports as 'a good class detached dwelling house' in quiet Gilberts Hill. They led the life of an ordinary family. Mr. Barrett, a company director, travelled to his office in London each week-day, whilst his wife would take the children to their school in Wendover, then return to her home and engage herself in various domestic activities until it was time to collect the children and prepare for her husband's homecoming.

There had been only one cloud in this idyllic setting and that had been the problem that faces many people who live in well to do areas, that of burglars, and in September of 1988 their house had been entered whilst Mrs. Barrett had been in the garden. Jewellery and a camera had been stolen and, despite all the work done by the Police, the perpetrator had not been caught. Upsetting though this was, life soon resumed its even tenor.

On Tuesday, 7th February 1989, Mr. Barrett left the house as usual for London. Shortly after Mrs. Barrett drove her children to school, returned to St. Leonards and then went to the parish church, where she helped to run the village play-group. At 12.30pm Mrs. Barrett, now back at home, spoke to someone on the telephone. It was shortly after that she answered a caller at the door.

At 4.45pm, when Mrs. Barrett had not called for her children, the headmistress of their school became anxious and contacted Mr. Barrett at his London office. He was somewhat mystified himself and in turn rang a friend, Richard Phillips, and asked him to call at the house to ascertain why Julia had not collected the children.

124

This Mr. Phillips did and, when he received no answer to his knocking on the door, he peered through a window and noticed a handbag on the floor with some credit cards strewn around. He forced open the window, clambered in and made his way cautiously around the house. As he entered the dining room he saw that something terrible had taken place, for lying face down was the body of Mrs. Barrett with a knife in her back!

She had been subjected to a brutal attack; a subsequent post-mortem revealed that she had sustained 31 wounds to her head, which had resulted in a fractured skull and a broken jaw, plus further injuries to neck and chest. There were additional defensive cuts to her forearm and hands, where she had tried to fend off her attacker, and there was an airgun pellet embedded in her head. She had also been beaten, kicked and trodden upon.

The local Police attended in the first instance, and Detective Superintendent Miller arrived to take overall charge of the investigation of this foul crime.

The house had been ransacked, but the most obvious thing to have been stolen was Mrs. Barrett's Ford Fiesta car. A thorough search of the house by the Police revealed a bloodstained poker, which appeared to have been used as a weapon during the ferocious attack upon Mrs. Barrett.

Enquiries were made at the houses in this normally quiet village, in the hope that someone might have seen something suspicious. Uniformed Police were drafted in to conduct a search in the immediate vicinity of the Barrett house. They discovered, in one of the many woods around St. Leonards, a mountain bike which had been reported stolen from Chesham. Whether it had any significance at that stage was not known.

Teams of detectives interviewed anyone who might have had any connections, however tenuous, with the Barretts. One of those seen was a seventeen-year-old youth, Martin Stevens, who lived at Chesham and who was employed by the local firm that had been engaged in carrying out the renovations at the Barrett house the previous autumn. Initially he told the detectives that he had been searching for his brother's stolen mountain bike; the same one that the Police had found near the house. When he was asked to detail his whereabouts during the afternoon of February 7th, he informed them that he had been with his employer until 2 pm, which the detectives found very interesting because that gentleman, when interviewed, stated quite categorically that Stevens had left at 12.20pm! Stevens had not only a discrepancy of slightly over an hour and a half to account for but, what was more important, why had he chosen to lie to the investigating officers? The detectives pressed him for a reply and they watched as Stevens first blushed, then began to cry. He admitted that he had called at the Barrett home that afternoon and, when he was asked why he had done so, he replied, "To get the car."

He was arrested, and as a matter of course his bedroom was searched. It was discovered that Stevens kept a diary and parts of it made very interesting reading, for in it he had written how he had worked at the Barrett's house and how nice it was and what nice things they had. He had also noted the times Mrs. Barrett had left to fetch the children from school. The detectives read on and saw that Stevens had written, '...wait in woods, watched her go. Run up the road to door, usual way in. Twenty minutes to get what I want.' Another diary entry recorded, 'I want the car so I've made a plan.' It was a plan to shoot Mrs. Barrett in the temple and this is what Stevens had actually done with his air pistol!

Stevens recounted to the detectives how he had gone to the house on the pretext of checking the earlier plastering work he had carried out. Once he was inside the house Mrs. Barrett had made him a cup of tea and had then started to telephone her husband to check what Stevens had told her was true. It was at that point that Stevens said that he had attacked her.

He was charged with the murder of Julia Barrett and in January 1990 pleaded guilty at Reading Crown Court. Mr. Justice McKinnon, in ordering him to be detained at Her Majesty's Pleasure, commented, "You are clearly a dangerous individual. In time it is to be hoped you will change."

Index